POWER BLENDER
REVOLUTION

POWER BLENDER
REVOLUTION

More Than 300 Healthy & Amazing Recipes That Unlock the Full Potential of Your Vitamix®, Blendtec®, Ninja®, or Other High-Speed, High-Power Blender

VANESSA SIMKINS

Author of *The Juice Lover's Big Book of Juices*

HARVARD COMMON PRESS

Brimming with creative inspiration, how-to projects, and useful
information to enrich your everyday life, Quarto Knows is a favorite
destination for those pursuing their interests and passions. Visit our
site and dig deeper with our books into your area of interest:
Quarto Creates, Quarto Cooks, Quarto Homes, Quarto Lives,
Quarto Drives, Quarto Explores, Quarto Gifts, or Quarto Kids.

First Published in 2018 by The Harvard Common Press, an imprint of The Quarto Group,
100 Cummings Center, Suite 265-D, Beverly, MA 01915, USA.
T (978) 282-9590 F (978) 283-2742 QuartoKnows.com

The Harvard Common Press titles are also available at discount for retail, wholesale, promotional, and bulk
purchase. For details, contact the Special Sales Manager by email at specialsales@quarto.com or by mail at The
Quarto Group, Attn: Special Sales Manager, 401 Second Avenue North, Suite 310, Minneapolis, MN 55401, USA.

22 21 20 19 18   1 2 3 4 5

ISBN: 978-1-55832-888-4

Library of Congress Cataloging-in-Publication Data is available

Page Layout: Sporto
Photography: Vanessa Simkins, except pages 20 and 280, Jessica Sunshine Christian

Printed in China

The effects of the ingredients and recipes in this book on health and wellness will vary from person to person.
There are many variables that play a role in your health. Always consult a physician about your health, wellness,
medical conditions, and dietary needs. Always consult with your doctor on any health questions, reactions, or
concerns you may have regarding the effects of ingredients and recipes. Recipes and advice are not meant to
cure, treat, or diagnose health issues or diseases. The health-related information provided in this work is based on
the author's research on nutrition and on her personal experience.

DEDICATION

To my family, my friends, and my *All About Juicing* family:
This book is dedicated to you. Without your love and
support, this wouldn't be possible, and I'm
eternally grateful you are all in my life.

CONTENTS

BLENDING POWERFULLY: AN INTRODUCTION

The power blender is one of the most-used appliances in my kitchen, and it's about to become yours, too. High-speed blenders are powerful and versatile. They'll make smoothies, ice cream, and everything in between. They're a true gem in the kitchen that can be your savior in a moment's notice.

I have big plans for you and this book. They go something like this:

You're about to get home to make your family dinner. You're not sure what to make, but you need something quick. Then, you remember your blender. You whip up a fresh lemon and olive oil vinaigrette dressing, and you pour it over a big bowl of kale salad. Then, you make a piping hot broccoli and cheese soup in under ten minutes. After you've eaten this healthy and light dinner, you feel like dessert. You rinse your blender and throw in some frozen strawberries and blend your way to an amazing, refreshingly sweet strawberry sorbet.

Before bed, you remember that you aren't going to have much time for breakfast. So, you whip up a quick smoothie with your blender and place it in the fridge to quickly grab the next day.

Now, doesn't that sound like a great plan for dinner and dessert plus breakfast? Your life is so much more manageable with this versatile machine.

We can make so many wonderful recipes in the power blender. I'm going to teach you how to do that, and it's quicker and cheaper than you'd imagine. This book will take you through all you need to know about making healthy recipes with your power blender. And if you're a blending veteran, you'll take away some fantastic recipes to use for a lifetime.

You'll learn how to use your blender to:

- grind homemade flours and grains
- chop cheese
- churn butter
- whip cream
- grind coffee
- make your own condiments
- whip up homemade salad dressings and marinades
- make soups
- make quick desserts

- make breakfast, lunch, and dinner with your blender

- make quick baby food

- use your blender to speed up making baked goods

- make homemade, toxic-free skin care

The recipes are fresh (and sometimes even decadent), and they can be made in a flash. They'll show you the amazing difference in quality between store-bought brands and recipes that you'll make yourself—recipes that everyone will love and ask for again and again. Using your blender, you can easily reduce unnecessary sugar, salt, and preservatives in your diet. You can also use your blender to cut down on prep time and cleanup time by efficiently preparing your ingredients in less time and with fewer kitchen tools. Many of the recipes also have serving tips to make you look like a super chef or an entertaining whiz and blending tips to ensure you're getting the most from your machine.

BENEFITS OF USING A POWER BLENDER

The power blender is a complete workhorse in the kitchen, and it also has many additional benefits that will be reflected in other areas of your life. As you use it frequently, you'll realize how it can be truly life changing.

- You can save time by using your power blender. It requires less effort to make recipes, compared to others that use many complicated applications. It also is a breeze to clean—just rinse and you're done. If you don't want to use the stovetop or oven, that's no problem. Just use the blender to make a meal instead.

- You can control the ingredients that go into your recipes and your body. When you make recipes, you don't have to worry about preservatives, chemicals, and corn syrup making it into your meals.

- You can make your own homemade ice cream, sauces, or salad dressings the way you want them to taste, not like a manufacturer made them. And you can make them without oils that you prefer not to consume. You'll love being able to tweak your favorite recipes to your liking and avoid made-in-the-lab flavorings.

- You can do things in one machine that you previously needed other tools for. The versatility of the blender is impressive. If you don't want to buy a separate food processor, coffee grinder, and stand mixer because you have a small space or simply don't want extra appliances filling your cabinets, the power blender covers you in all those areas. It makes it perfect for an efficient kitchen, and it is useful in small spaces, such as a college dorm or a vacation home. It's also great for traveling when you'll be cooking a few meals, but you'll have minimal space for tools.

HOW TO USE THIS BOOK

There are a lot of different power blenders on the market and more are hitting the shelves each day. You'll want to know how to work your machine, and be sure to read through your user's manual before starting to use it. Some have dials to control speed and some have preset buttons. Others won't be as powerful as high-end models, and you'll have to adapt the recipes by blending in batches or adding more liquid. Some come with tampers and several blades and others don't. Either way, all of these recipes can be made in any power blender, but you should know how to work yours and use your own judgment when operating it for each recipe.

Throughout this book, I'll provide you with tips within the chapters so you can make the most of your prep time and your machine. I've also included tips about how to serve the recipe and what pairs well with it. Most of these recipes can be made very quickly—within minutes. I don't like spending a lot of time in the kitchen for one recipe, so if a recipe took longer than I'd like, it was tossed. In some cases, you'll find even more shortcuts to cut time, such as using frozen fruits instead of adding ice or using precooked cauliflower for your cauliflower mash. Take note of the order that I suggest adding the ingredients to your blender, as I've found this optimal for processing. I encourage you to save time where you can in the kitchen and get creative in using your machine.

Recipes can be tweaked to your own liking. If you don't like all the ingredients or spices I'm using, feel free to come up with your own versions. In fact, I hope you have fun and make these recipes your own—that's part of the joy of cooking and of spending time in the kitchen.

I believe that there is beauty in most diets and ways of eating. Over the years, I've experimented with many styles of eating to find my perfect fit for me and my family. What may work for you may not work for others. I hold true to these three things: First, clean eating is important to good health. Second, healthy fats are a must for our bodies. Third, vegetables and fruits are an important, versatile part of our diets.

You'll find the recipes in this book are free of anything processed. It's all clean, pure food using a lot of fresh fruits and vegetables. You'll also see that I am not afraid of using healthy fats. I do not believe fat makes us fat—our bodies need it to function optimally. Because we all have different diets, I've included a wide array of recipes to suit your needs, as well as ways to meet the needs of your family and friends. In some recipes, I use dairy or gluten-free flour. Some recipes might use honey, while others use stevia. This might be to your liking or maybe it's not. Feel free to switch out whatever ingredient works better for you, your needs, and the seasonal availability of ingredients. Make the recipe to your ideal taste.

If you're health conscious or if you are cooking for those with restrictions and allergies, I've indicated if recipes are vegan, gluten-free, dairy-free, nut-free, or low-sugar.

(V) Vegan: A Vegan recipe is one that is free of any animal products, including meat, dairy, animal broth, and honey, or it can be made that way based on the options.

(GF) Gluten-Free: This means that the recipe is free of gluten and gluten-containing ingredients.

(DF) Dairy-Free: This indicates the recipe is free of any animal dairy ingredients. Note that if a recipe does contain dairy, you can always easily switch it out with your favorite nondairy substitute, many of which I give you recipes for in this book in the Nondairy Milks chapter (page 74).

(NF) Nut-Free: Nut-free recipes indicate that no items in the nut family are present in the recipe.

(LS) Low-Sugar: When a recipe indicates it's low in sugar, it doesn't mean that there is zero sugar in the nutritional content. Rather, it means that no added sugars in the form of cane or coconut sugar, dates, honey, maple syrup, agave, and the like are present in the recipe.

I know that the blender will rock your world if you give it a good chance. My wish is that you'll save time, money, and effort in the kitchen with this one amazing appliance, just as I have. Fresh, healthy, and delicious meals are coming your way. Enjoy!

POWER BLENDER TOOLS AND ACCESSORIES

To make delicious blended foods, your blender is the star of the show and you don't need much else but your recipe ingredients. However, here are some additional tools that

I use in my kitchen when making blender-centric meals, making the job easier and more efficient.

Nut Milk Bag A nut milk bag is one of those tools you want to have in your kitchen to accompany your blender. You can use it for making pulp-free milks and pulp-free juices, and you can even strain cheeses, butter, and other things that require a fine strain. They typically are made of a nylon fabric which will catch any grittiness. I use mine much more than I anticipated when I purchased one. Alternatively, you can use a fine-mesh strainer in place of a nut milk bag. You might prefer this if you're making classic butter or if you prefer pouring the mixture over a bowl to strain versus squeezing the pulp from a nut milk bag, which can be more labor intensive.

Spatulas Spatulas are absolutely necessary for scooping out, mixing, and pushing down ingredients in your blender container. I prefer the silicone versions as these gently scrape the sides to remove every last drop from the container.

Scales, Measuring Cups, and Measuring Spoons While most blender containers have measuring units that you can use at times, scales and measuring utensils are necessary for making a successful and accurate recipe in your machine.

Tampers Some machines come with built-in tampers and some don't. If you have the option of getting one, it's a great tool to own. The tamper helps ease the flow when blending the product. It's often that you'll have to stop the machine and push down ingredients to finish blending the recipe. If you have a tamper, it makes it much easier to push the ingredients into the blades while blending and to fully combine the recipe.

Cutting Board and Knives A good set of knives and a sturdy cutting board are essential to creating the perfect blended food. These will help you prepare your ingredients properly before placing them in your blender.

Bowls It's quite often you'll need a bowl to premix or transfer a mixture from your blender to another area to finish out the recipe. They also come in handy when straining nut milks and juices.

ESSENTIAL ADVICE FOR POWER-BLENDING

A power blender is durable and tough, but not indestructible. If you treat it with respect, it will make a huge difference in how your recipes turn out, and it will go a long way to preserving the life of your appliance. Because it's such a unique machine, there are a few special points you should know to help you through your recipes with ease. Here's what I've learned over the years to take my recipes to a new level and operate my machine with simplicity.

Layering Ingredients It's often helpful to place ingredients in your blender in an order that will help it to process more efficiently. In many recipes, it's optimal to add liquids first, then small and light items, and then larger, heavier items. Liquids, such as water or broth, as the bottom layer will help to lift the ingredients off the blades and bring down the rest of the ingredients into a spiral, ensuring the machine doesn't clog.

Layer one: Liquids, such as water, broth, or milk

Layer two: Small and lighter items, such as spices, powders, and chopped vegetables and fruits

Layer three: Heavy and large items, such as frozen fruits and ice

While these rules of layering are not essential (and they definitely do not apply in all cases), they do help troubleshoot problems if you notice your blender tends to clog when blending recipes. This layering technique will quickly become second nature to you as you get used to your machine.

Control the Speed Pulsing your machine or blending on low is the best way to start blending a recipe. This helps the mixture to get moving and gently combine the ingredients, avoiding clogs. Once you combine your recipe ingredients on low speed or by pulsing, you can continue to blend on medium or high with ease, if needed.

Use the Tamper If your machine comes with a tamper, don't be nervous to use it. The tamper is designed to be used when the machine is on. It will not touch the blades. It aids in pushing the ingredients into the blades and helps the mixture move more efficiently. Note: If a tamper did not come with your blender, do not use a spatula or spoon when the machine is running or you will ruin your recipe (and potentially the blender blades). Stop your machine first and then use a spatula to scrape the sides and redistribute the mixture.

Expect Noise One thing that often shocks high-power blending rookies is that it's extremely loud when blending, especially when making recipes with frozen ingredients or a small amount of liquid. This is common and nothing to fear. The beauty of your high-powered blender is that it can do many powerful things, but the noise is just part of the process when doing its job.

Chop, Mince, and Grate Your blender is powerful, but that doesn't mean you won't ever need to chop, mince, or grate fibrous or harder foods to help your blender process ingredients. Keep in mind that not every dish you make with your blender must be completely smooth. To achieve different textures, you must chop, mince, and grate, and you'll need to use the speed control wisely. Being thoughtful in this area will help reduce stress on your blender's motor, and it also will ensure the proper texture of your finished dish.

Consider Soaking While not always necessary, it's a great idea to soak nuts, seeds, and dried fruits and vegetables before blending, especially if there is a minimal amount of liquids in the recipe. This will reduce stress on your machine and ensure a velvety smooth, even texture in your finished recipe.

Use Seasonings Sparingly When seasonings are processed through high-powered blender blades their essential oils and flavors are spread more thoroughly and noticeably through the mix. When seasoning recipes to your liking, be sure to keep it in mind that a little goes a long way. It's better to use less and test than to add too much and ruin your dish.

Be Careful with Hot Liquids Most high-powered blenders are designed to handle very hot temperatures. It's helpful to use your blender to puree foods after cooking them,

such as soups or hot side dishes. While it's undoubtedly an efficient way to use your machine, know that hot liquids expand when blended, so you'll never want to fill the container completely if your mixture is very hot. For best results in most recipes, fill your blender container only halfway to the top and start out at the lowest speed, slowly increasing to higher speeds. The safest way to blend is to let it cool a bit and remove the small center lid cap to let steam escape. Additionally, hot and cold extremes dull our taste buds, so letting it cool will help you get better results when taste testing.

Always Secure the Lid While it's tempting to not secure the lid before blending some recipes, it's a good idea to make this a habit at all times. Your blender is mighty, and the ingredients will swirl with intensity as soon as you turn it on. Always put the lid on your blender container and secure it before blending to avoid explosions and unnecessary cleaning in your kitchen.

Don't Overload It's tempting to pack as much as you can into your blender container, but blenders work best when you leave sufficient room at the top to allow the mixture to expand and swirl. Try to never fill your container more than three-quarters full of ingredients. It's best to blend in batches and transfer the finished, blended mixture into a bowl or pot while you complete the rest of your recipe.

Don't Overheat When blending extra-thick blends, such as pastes, spreads, nut butters, and dips, it's best to process in short bursts of about 20 to 30 seconds to prevent overheating and clogging your machine. If you hear your motor struggling or it appears the blades have stopped spinning, it's likely the mixture is trapped in an air bubble or too thick to process. The ingredients will most likely need to be shifted. Stop the machine, open the lid, and use a spatula to redistribute the mixture around the container. Adding extra liquid can also make a huge difference to get the mixture moving again when this happens.

Clean the Machine An easy way to achieve quick cleanup with your blender is to fill it halfway full with cold water and add a few drops of dish soap. Place the blender container back on your blender base, with the lid secured tightly, and blend on high for a few seconds until you see the ingredients lifting from the side of the container. Stop the machine and take it back to the sink to dump the water. Finally, rinse out the blender container with clean, fresh water. Do this immediately after using so ingredients don't have a chance to dry or set up in the container, which can be hard to remove. This will save you time scrubbing with a sponge and damaging your container. In most cases, it works like magic to clean your machine in mere seconds.

SPECIAL TECHNIQUES FOR THE POWER BLENDER

The power blender can help you out in the kitchen in several ways to make your life extra easy. Here are some unique features you might want to use to make the most out of your machine.

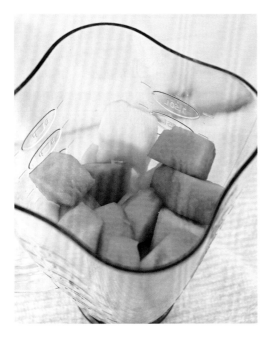

HOMEMADE FLOURS AND OTHER MILLED GRAINS

It's often easier and cheaper to buy a large package of whole grains in bulk if you use them often. If you have a package of whole grains on hand that you'd like to mill into flour, your blender can easily do this task. It has worked with any grain I've tried, from rice to millet to quinoa. To make your own flour, add the grain to your blender container. You'll want to pulse the blender at first. Then, blend on high, stopping often to push down particles on the side that have not yet blended. Do this until you reach a flour consistency.

GRINDING AND CHOPPING CHEESE

I find that the power blender is excellent for grating and chopping cheeses of all types. Hard cheeses, such as Parmesan, for example, grind extremely well. Medium hard cheeses, such as sharp Cheddar, also chop well, and this is helpful for those times when chopped cheese will melt into a recipe easier. I frequently buy large chunks of cheese at big box retailers and make my own grated cheese at home. It's quite a time-saver compared to cutting or grating your own on a grater. To grind or chop your own cheese, you'll want to make sure you cut the cheese into small chunks, at least 1-inch (2.5 cm) thick, before placing it in the blender container. Once you've hand-chopped the cheese and placed it in your blender, pulse the blender at first until the cheese is broken up into small chunks. Continue to blend until you've reached your desired consistency.

WET CHOPPING VEGETABLES

Power blenders can wet chop vegetables with ease, and this can really be a time-saver for recipes like coleslaw where you'd normally have to pull out your food processor or hand

chop the cabbage. While you can chop any vegetable straight in the blender, the best technique is to generously fill your blender with water a few inches (about 7 cm) from the top and add large chunks of the vegetable. You'll want to blend quickly and stop quickly. When you turn it on, you'll notice the water helps to buffer the chop so that the vegetable doesn't turn to mush. Be sure to watch it closely and not leave it running, or it will blend the vegetable into the water. If you want to experiment with this technique, try it on cabbage first.

GRINDING MEAT

Grinding meats such as chicken, pork, turkey, or beef can be a real problem if you don't have a special meat grinder. Your power blender can help you out in this area, too. There are two ways to grind meat, and depending on your blender, you'll have to experiment with which one works best for your machine.

Method #1: Cut your meat into 1-inch (2.5 cm) cubes. Remove the lid cap and start your machine on medium-low. While it's on, drop in the meat cubes, one by one, in 20 second increments. Stop often to remove the already chopped meat so that it doesn't overgrind. If adding spices, transfer the meat to a bowl and hand mix the seasonings in with a spatula.

Method #2: Cut your meat into 1-inch (2.5 cm) cubes. Place about ¼ pound (115 g) of meat into your blender container. If adding spices, add them to the meat. Pulse or blend on low, quickly creating a pulse motion to grind the meat, using a tamper and stopping often to gently mix with a spatula to redistribute the mixture.

WHIPPING CREAM

Whipping cream can be done very quickly in your blender and makes for quick and easy desserts. To whip cream, add heavy whipping cream plus any sugar or sugar substitutes or extracts into your blender container. Blend on high until well combined and thickened.

You'll want to stop the machine and push down the cream after your first blending to make sure it's all combined. Do not let it blend very long or it will turn into sweet butter. If you'd like a vegetarian version of whipping cream, follow the directions for whipping heavy cream but use coconut cream taken from the top of a chilled can of full-fat coconut milk.

CHURNING BUTTERS

Making your own butter from scratch is very time-consuming if you do it by hand, but with your power blender, you can make it quickly and easily in minutes. And as a bonus, it's fun to experiment with making flavored butters. To make your own butter, you'll want to add heavy whipping cream and salt into your blender container. Blend on high until well combined. Stop the blender to push down any cream that splattered at the top of the container. Continue to blend until it becomes thick, and you can see that it has turned into butter. To make flavored butters, you can add flavorings to start, or you can make the plain butter and add in the mix-ins —such as fresh parsley, garlic, or pink salt— and mix it in a bowl. Wrap a roll of butter in parchment paper and twist it at the end. Store it in your refrigerator until ready to use.

CRUSHING ICE

If you'd like crushed ice and your freezer does not make it, then the power blender can do it quickly for you. To make crushed ice, add ice cubes into your blender container. Pulse the blender until it has reached your desired crush. If you blend on high, it will blend it into a very fine ice, which can be used for snow cones or frozen drinks.

GRINDING COFFEE

Grinding coffee can be problematic if you don't have a coffee grinder, but the power blender can do this in minutes. To grind coffee, add whole dry roasted beans to your blender container. Pulse until your reach your desired consistency, stopping halfway through to scrape down the sides.

MAKING HOT SOUPS AND COCOAS

Certain blender models can make soups and cocoas piping hot, allowing you to skip using the stove to heat up your meal or drink. You'll want to check with the manufacturer and your specific model manual to see if yours has this capability. Currently, the Vitamix and the Blendtec are the most popular models that have this feature. To make hot soups or cocoas, you'll want to blend the recipe on the highest setting for seven to ten minutes until you see it is hot. It will be loud. When it's ready and you open the lid, be careful because the steam escapes and it is very hot.

POWDERING SUGAR

Often, you might have a recipe that calls for powdered sugar, but you only have granular sugar. The power blender can help you here, too. I find this feature works well with regular cane and coconut sugar, as well as alternative sweeteners such as xylitol or erythritol. To make powdered sugar, simply add the granular sugar into your blender container. Blend on high for about a minute or until you see that it has powdered.

GRINDING SPICE BLENDS

Making your own spices from scratch proves rewarding, and it's easy to do with your blender. Pick whole spices and the ratio at which you'd like to create a specific flavor profile. Add them to your blender container and blend until it becomes a fine powder. Store in airtight glass containers, and if the spice blend is moist, allow it to dry for at least six hours on a plate before storing.

MAKING NUT BUTTERS

Nut butters are flavorful, and they are a great addition to most diets, but store-bought brands are expensive and often include undesirable added oils and sugar. I include several specific recipes in this book. The basic method for making your own nut butters is to simply blend your nuts of choice, using the tamper, in short bursts in your machine, taking great care to not overload or overheat the motor. If you find your machine will not turn over the nuts, add a small amount, 1 tablespoon (15 ml) at a time, of a healthful oil like coconut, olive, safflower, or sunflower to gently process the butter.

POWER BLENDER
7-DAY CLEAN EATING PLAN

If you have a limited amount of space and only a few appliances to use, the power blender can help you simplify your kitchen time and eat clean 24 hours a day, 7 days a week. It proves invaluable if you live in a small apartment, and it's great for when you're on vacation, in campers or on boats, in a college dorm room, or even in hotel rooms.

In this meal plan for 7 days of clean eating with your power blender, some recipes are made only with the help of your blender. Others require the use of other appliances, such as an oven or toaster oven, to complete the process. There are plenty of recipes in the book that only use the blender and nothing else, so if this is what you need, search by chapter to find what suits your situation best. Once you follow this guide, you'll get the hang of it. Before long, you'll be creating your own meal plans to use your blender.

DAY ONE

Breakfast: Green Grace Juice (page 43)

Lunch: Spinach salad with feta cheese and Watermelon Vinaigrette (page 162)

Dinner: Broccoli Cheddar Soup (page 178)

Snack/Dessert: Orange Mango Pudding (page 241)

DAY TWO

Breakfast: Chocolate Coconut Protein Muffins (page 221) with Coconut Creme Cafe (page 67)

Lunch: Chicken fajita bowl, with Salt-and-Pepper Cauliflower Rice (page 215) topped with sautéed onions, bell peppers, and grilled chicken

Dinner: Rice pasta with Cheddar Sauce (page 144) or Cauliflower Alfredo Sauce (page 136)

Snack/Dessert: Strawberry Sorbet (page 258)

DAY THREE

Breakfast: Maca Mango Paradise Smoothie (page 47)

Lunch: Falafel Patties (page 195) with Tahini Sauce (page 129) and Tabbouleh Salad (page 217)

Dinner: Sun-Dried Tomato and Roasted Red Pepper Soup (page 180)

Snack/Dessert: Piña Colada Chia Pudding (page 242) with fresh chopped fruit

DAY FOUR

Breakfast: Blueberry Almond Scones (page 224) with Whipped Honey Butter (page 94)

Lunch: Classic Tomato Soup (page 192) with Pao de Queso Cheese Rolls (page 238)

Dinner: Savory Chicken Pie (page 202) with Classic Coleslaw (page 211)

Snack/Dessert: Chocolate Mocha Fudge Popsicles (page 264)

DAY FIVE

Breakfast: Blueberry Pancakes (page 226) or Whole Wheat Waffles (page 227) with Blueberry Fruit Syrup (page 102) and Matcha Latte (page 71)

Lunch: Green leaf lettuce salad with chopped tomatoes, cucumbers, hard-boiled eggs, and Blue Cheese Dressing (page 166)

Dinner: Panfried Mushroom Ravioli (page 196) with Tomato Sauce (page 134)

Snack/Dessert: Watermelon Mint Slushie (page 64)

DAY SIX

Breakfast: Apple Cinnamon Smoothie Bowl (page 174)

Lunch: Zucchini and Pea Fritters (page 207) with Creamed Spinach (page 216)

Dinner: Shiitake Mushroom Bisque (page 183) and a side salad with Lemon Olive Oil Vinaigrette (page 156)

Snack/Dessert: Flourless Walnut Fudge Brownies (page 251)

DAY SEVEN

Breakfast: Broccoli and Cheese Frittata (page 230) or Banana Walnut Bread (page 234)

Lunch: Mashed Chickpea Lettuce Wrap (page 205)

Dinner: Cauliflower Crust Pizza (page 199) or Whole Wheat Margherita Pizza (page 197)

Snack/Dessert: Peanut Butter Banana Whip (page 262)

POWER BLENDER 3-DAY
JUICE AND SMOOTHIE CLEANSE

Because your blender can help you whip up delicious juices and smoothies, it's a true asset if you'd like to do a periodic juice cleanse. All liquid cleanses are very detoxing and healing for your body, but you'll want to do them right. Ease in 2 days before and 2 days after with light, clean, homemade meals to prepare your body for what's coming during the cleanse. Go easy when reintroducing heavier foods after the cleanse, too. I'll give you example meal ideas plus the juice menu to make it easy.

PRE-CLEANSE

- Get clear on your goals for the cleanse.

- Get into the mindset of cleaning out toxins from your body and supplying your body with nourishment.

- Get support from family and friends before you embark on your journey.

- Begin reducing processed foods, gluten, artificial sweeteners, alcohol, sugar, and caffeine.

- Look at any toxic relationships in your life, and see how you can reduce the time spent with toxic people.

- Clean out the cabinets, stock the fridge, and buy clean spring water and coconut water to hydrate in between drinking your juices and smoothies.

It's best to eat lightly and cleanly a few days before the cleanse to prepare your body and make the cleanse the best possible experience.

Here are some suggested meals for the 2 days before you start your cleanse.

BREAKFAST: Choose any smoothie or shake from the Smoothies chapter (page 46), any juice from the Whole Food Juices chapter (page 28), Vanilla Coconut Rice Cereal (page 230), a bowl of fresh chopped fruit, or any smoothie bowl from the Smoothie Bowls chapter (page 170).

If you are accustomed to having a lot of caffeine or coffee, try to have less and substitute it with the Matcha Latte (page 71).

LUNCHES AND DINNERS: Have soup, salads, or smoothie bowls for lunch and dinner meals.

Choose soups that are light, clean, and full of vegetables.

Good soup options: Pumpkin Soup (page 179), Sun-Dried Tomato and Roasted Red Pepper Soup (page 180), Coconut Cauliflower Soup (page 186), Ginger Carrot Soup (page 191), Classic Tomato Soup (page 192), Cucumber Yogurt Soup (page 179), Black Bean Soup (page 182), Vegetable Broth (page 193), and Watermelon Gazpacho (page 192)

Make a salad from leafy greens and your favorite chopped vegetables and dress it with a clean homemade dressing.

Good salad dressing options: Raspberry Walnut Vinaigrette (page 151), Carrot Miso Dressing (page 150), Strawberry Vinaigrette (page 150), Cucumber Herb Dressing (page 152), Cilantro Lime Dressing (page 152), Honey Mustard Vinaigrette (page 154), Red Pepper Dressing (page 155), Sweet Lemon

and Garlic Tahini Dressing (page 158), Green Goddess Ranch Dressing (page 159), Sesame Soy Vinaigrette (page 163), and Watermelon Vinaigrette (page 162)

DESSERTS: For desserts, choose light, fruit-based options such as Strawberry Sorbet (page 258), Vegan Banana Whip (page 261), Chocolate Mocha Fudge Popsicles (page 264), Coconut Lime Popsicles (page 265), Mixed Berry Sorbet (page 259), Pineapple Whip Sorbet (page 259), Watermelon Popsicles (page 265), and Vegan Mint Chip Ice Cream (page 263).

SNACKS: Fruit, cut-up vegetables with Carrot Hummus (page 114) or Beet Hummus (page 113) or Sweet Vegan Ranch Dressing (page 153), apples and celery with Honey Peanut Butter (page 97) or Honey Maple Almond Butter (page 98), and any nondairy milk from the Nondairy Milk chapter (page 74)

THE JUICE CLEANSE ROUTINE: DAYS 1–3

UPON WAKING: Drink 8 ounces (235 ml) of warm lemon water with 1 tablespoon (15 ml) of raw apple cider vinegar and a dash of sea salt. Feel free to add a tablespoon (20 g) of honey and a sprinkle of cayenne pepper or cinnamon.

Before showering, do skin brushing to support healthy detox, lymphatic flow, and boost your metabolism

THE JUICE MENU: Drink five juices daily, 12 to 16 ounces (355 to 475 ml) each. For an optimal cleanse and to make it easy, drink the juices in this order, each day of the cleanse.

9:00 a.m. Green Grace Juice (page 43)

11:00 a.m. Ginger Pear Paradise Juice (page 42)

1:00 p.m. Green Balancer Juice (page 41)

3:00 p.m. Carrot Lemonade Juice (page 32) or Red Sweetie Juice (page 42)

6:00 p.m. Cucumber Mint Cleanser Juice (page 35)

8:00 p.m. Grape Starlet Juice (page 40) (Add a handful of leafy greens to the recipe, if desired.)

Feel free to switch up any of the greens in these juices with kale, green leaf lettuce, romaine lettuce, arugula, or spinach to give your body variety and extra nutrition.

Stay hydrated throughout the day with water. Add a smoothie (page 46). Good options include: Green Bliss Smoothie (page 47), Strawberry Shortcake Smoothie (page 51), Green Goddess Smoothie (page 48), or Whole Food Juice (page 28). Make Vegetable Broth (page 193) or other vegetable-based soup if needed for extra nourishment or if you feel weak.

POST-CLEANSE

Because your body has been having liquid nourishment for the past few days, it's important to come off the cleanse in a gentle way and not eat big, heavy meals to disrupt your system. You can eat a little heavier than you did pre-cleanse as you reintroduce foods.

Here are some suggested meals for the 2 days following the cleanse

UPON WAKING: Drink 8 ounces (235 ml) of warm lemon water with 1 tablespoon (15 ml) of raw apple cider vinegar and a dash of sea salt. Feel free to add a tablespoon (20 g) of honey and a sprinkle of cayenne pepper or cinnamon.

BREAKFAST: Choose any smoothie or shake from the Smoothies chapter (page 46), any juice from the Whole Food Juices chapter (page 28), Vanilla Coconut Rice Cereal (page

230), Gluten-Free Banana Bread (page 232), a bowl of fresh chopped fruit, or any smoothie bowl from the Smoothie Bowls chapter (page 70).

Substitute coffee with the Matcha Latte (page 71).

LUNCHES AND DINNERS: Have soup, salads, or smoothie bowls for lunch and dinner meals.

Choose soups that are light, clean, and full of vegetables.

Good soup options: Pumpkin Soup (page 179), Sun-Dried Tomato and Roasted Red Pepper Soup (page 180), Coconut Cauliflower Soup (page 186), Ginger Carrot Soup (page

191), Classic Tomato Soup (page 192), Cucumber Yogurt Soup (page 179), Black Bean Soup (page 182), Vegetable Broth (page 193), Watermelon Gazpacho (page 192), Cream of Asparagus Soup (page 182), Creamy Corn Chowder (page 184), and Shiitake Mushroom Bisque (page 183)

Make a salad from leafy greens and your favorite chopped vegetables and dress it with a clean homemade dressing.

Good salad dressing options: Raspberry Walnut Vinaigrette (page 151), Carrot Miso Dressing (page 150), Strawberry Vinaigrette (page 150), Cucumber Herb Dressing (page 152), Cilantro Lime Dressing (page 152), Honey Mustard Vinaigrette (page 154), Red Pepper Dressing (page 155), Sweet Lemon and Garlic Tahini Dressing (page 158), Green Goddess Ranch Dressing (page 159), Sesame Soy Vinaigrette (page 163), Watermelon Vinaigrette (page 162), and Maple Balsamic Vinaigrette (page 157)

DESSERTS: For desserts, choose light, fruit-based options such as Strawberry Sorbet (page 258), Vegan Banana Whip (page 261), Chocolate Mocha Fudge Popsicles (page 264), Coconut Lime Popsicles (page 265), Mixed Berry Sorbet (page 259), Pineapple Whip Sorbet (page 259), Watermelon Popsicles (page 265), and Vegan Mint Chip Ice Cream (page 263).

SNACKS: Fruit, cut-up vegetables with Carrot Hummus (page 114), Beet Hummus (page 113), Sweet Vegan Ranch Dressing (page 153), Almond Hummus (page 112), Creamy Guacamole (page 116), or Tropical Guacamole (page 115), apples and celery with Honey Peanut Butter (page 97) or Honey Maple Almond Butter (page 98), and any nondairy milk from the Nondairy Milk chapter (page 74)

Continue to stay hydrated and drink homemade nut milks (page 74) if you wish. If you feel you need to snack during your post-cleanse, have a piece of fruit, a handful of seeds, nuts, a smoothie (page 46), or some Vegetable Broth (page 193).

After day two of the post-cleanse, you'll want to slowly reintroduce grains, if you desire, by having a bowl of oatmeal with fruit or gluten-free bread with Sun-Dried Tomato Spread (page 106), Strawberry Chia Jam (page 91), or Cashew Butter (page 96). If you are reintroducing proteins, try scrambled eggs with Fresh Tomato Salsa (page 108) and salads with homemade dressing and cleanly sourced chicken or fish.

Now that you have felt the benefits of juicing, you can continue to incorporate juicing and smoothies into your life for hydration, cellular detoxification, and pure liquid energy.

THE RECIPES

PART 1:

THINGS TO DRINK

1

WHOLE FOOD
JUICES

If you're in need of a hydrating and nutritious juice, there's no quicker way to whip up a blended juice than with ripe, juicy produce and your trusty blender. Whole food juices allow you to reap the benefits of the vitamins and minerals from fresh produce plus the added fiber. They're also lighter and juicier than their thick and creamy smoothie counterparts. These combinations are just what you need when you want both something that's nutritious and delicious. Bottoms up!

Cantaloupe Crush Juice

Makes 12 to 16 ounces (355 to 475 ml)

This juice is the perfect summertime drink. It's naturally sweet, hydrating, and super healthy for a relaxing day in the sun. I think this has a perfect sweetness all on its own, but add stevia, honey or agave if you prefer.

1 cup (155 g) chopped cantaloupe, rind removed
1 cup (155 g) chopped pineapple, rind removed
½ cup (120 ml) cold water
¼ cup (60 ml) crushed ice
5 drops of liquid stevia extract or ½ table-spoon (10 g) honey or agave (optional)

1. Add the cantaloupe, pineapple, water, and ice to your blender container.

2. Blend on high until smooth, just a few seconds. Taste and see if you'd like additional sweetener. Add if desired, blending once more.

3. If you'd like a very smooth, pulp-free juice, strain the mixture over a medium-size bowl through a nut milk bag or fine-mesh strainer before serving. Serve immediately.

> ☞ **BLENDING TIP**
>
> Don't ever blend the rind or peels of produce in your blender. They are not edible and might damage your machine.

Blueberry Pear Magic Juice

Makes 12 to 16 ounces (355 to 475 ml)

You'll never taste the spinach, only the pear and blueberries, in this magical juice drink that transforms into a lovely shade of purple.

1 cored and chopped d'Anjou pear, about 1½ cups (242 g) chopped
½ cup (75 g) blueberries
½ cup (15 g) spinach
½ cup (120 ml) cold coconut water
¼ cup (60 ml) crushed ice
3 drops of liquid stevia extract or ½ table-spoon (10 g) honey or agave (optional)

1. Add the pear, blueberries, spinach, coconut water, and ice to your blender container.

2. Blend on high until smooth and the spinach and blueberries have completely combined, about 15 seconds. Taste and see if you'd like sweetener. Add if desired, blending once more.

3. If you'd like a very smooth, pulp-free juice, strain the mixture over a medium-size bowl through a nut milk bag or fine-mesh strainer before serving. Serve immediately.

◀ Coco Green Juice

Makes 12 to 16 ounces (355 to 475 ml)

This orange-spiked coconut juice is an easy way to consume your daily greens, and it is refreshingly light and full of nourishing vitamins to fuel your day. Boost this juice with a handful or two of greens if you don't mind the flavor. Be patient when blending; it will take some time for the kale to blend because this is a very juicy juice.

(V) (GF) (DF) (NF) (LS)

1 large orange, peeled and halved
1 cup (67 g) baby kale
1 cup (235 ml) cold coconut water
Ice cubes for serving (optional)

1. Add the orange, kale, and coconut water to your blender container.

2. Blend on high until smooth and the kale is blended.

3. If you'd like a very smooth, pulp-free juice, strain the mixture over a medium-size bowl through a nut milk bag or fine-mesh strainer before serving. Serve immediately over ice, if desired.

☞ **TIP**

You can use any variety of kale in your blended juices, but baby kale is delicate and blends better into a watery juice. Save the mature and denser kale varieties for your creamier and thicker smoothies.

Green Pineapple Party Juice

Makes 12 to 16 ounces (355 to 475 ml)

This is a great way to combine romaine lettuce in blended juices; the pineapple hides the green taste nicely. If you aren't used to greens in your drinks, you may want to add stevia extract, honey or agave to sweeten the flavor.

1 cup (155 g) chopped pineapple, rind removed
1 medium orange, peeled and halved
1 large romaine lettuce leaf, about 1 cup (47 g) chopped
½ cup (120 ml) cold water
¼ cup (60 ml) crushed ice
3 drops of liquid stevia extract or ½ tablespoon (10 g) honey or agave (optional)

1. Add the pineapple, orange, romaine lettuce, water, and ice to your blender container.

2. Blend on high until smooth and the romaine lettuce has fully combined. Taste and see if you'd like additional sweetener. Add if desired, blending once more.

3. If you'd like a very smooth, pulp-free juice, strain the mixture over a medium-size bowl through a nut milk bag or fine-mesh strainer before serving. Serve immediately.

Carrot Lemonade Juice ▶

Makes 12 to 16 ounces (355 to 475 ml)

Bursting with lemon flavor, this extremely refreshing drink is full of beta carotene. It's the ultimate way to chug naturally sweet carrots and reap the cleansing benefits of lemons.

1 chopped carrot, about ½ cup (65 g)
1 cored and chopped small green apple, about 1 cup (125 g)
1 peeled and halved lemon
1 cup (235 ml) cold coconut water
½ cup (120 ml) crushed ice
5 drops of liquid stevia extract or 1 tablespoon (20 g) honey or agave (optional)

1. Add the carrot, apple, lemon, coconut water, and ice to your blender container.

2. Blend on high until smooth and the carrots have fully blended. Taste and see if you'd like additional sweetener. Add if desired, blending once more.

3. If you'd like a very smooth, pulp-free juice, strain the mixture over a medium-size bowl through a nut milk bag or fine-mesh strainer before serving. Serve immediately.

Pink Summer Juice ▶

Makes 12 to 16 ounces (355 to 475 ml)

This simple blend helps to remove water weight from your body and is extremely hydrating. Enjoy it when summertime temperatures are rising. It's not overly sweet, but I love it that way.

**2 cups (300 g) chopped watermelon,
  rind removed**
½ of a peeled lemon
1 chopped celery stalk, about ¼ cup (25 g)
½ cup (120 ml) cold water
½ cup (120 ml) crushed ice
5 drops of liquid stevia extract
**1 tablespoon (20 g) honey or agave
  (optional)**

1. Add the watermelon, lemon, celery, water, ice, and stevia extract to your blender container.

2. Blend on high until smooth or until the celery has fully combined. Taste and see if you'd like additional sweetener. Add if desired, blending once more.

3. If you'd like a very smooth, pulp-free juice, strain the mixture over a medium-size bowl through a nut milk bag or fine-mesh strainer before serving. Serve immediately.

☞ BLENDING TIP

Juicy fruits, such as melons and citrus, work best in whole food blender juice. When making your own juice recipes, combine juicy fruits with less juicy fruits to reduce the amount of liquid needed for blending. If you use only juicy fruits, you will not need much liquid in the blend.

Strawberry Pineapple Lemonade Juice

Makes 12 to 16 ounces (355 to 475 ml)

Make this sour strawberry-pineapple juice for a midafternoon treat. If you are a lemon lover, this will make you pucker with delight. Stevia extract works well to naturally sweeten and reduce the sourness of the lemon. If you prefer to lessen the lemon pucker even more, add honey or agave to the blend.

1 cup (155 g) chopped pineapple, rind removed
1 small peeled lemon
½ cup (85 g) chopped strawberries
½ cup (120 ml) cold coconut water
½ cup (120 ml) crushed ice
8 drops of liquid stevia extract
½ tablespoon (10 g) honey or agave (optional)
Ice cubes for serving

1. Add the pineapple, lemon, strawberries, coconut water, ice, and stevia extract to your blender container.

2. Blend on high until smooth and fully combined. Taste and see if you'd like additinal sweetener. Add if desired, blending once more.

3. If you'd like a very smooth, pulp-free juice, strain the mixture over a medium-size bowl through a nut milk bag or fine-mesh strainer before serving. Serve immediately over ice.

Cucumber Mint Cleanser Juice

Makes 12 to 16 ounces (355 to 475 ml)

Green is in, and once you taste this juice, you'll be so excited you hopped on this bandwagon too. This blend combines beautifully to give you a nutrient-rich drink that makes you proud to drink green and delighted to share it with others.

½ of a chopped cucumber, about ½ cup (70 g)
1 cored and chopped Granny Smith apple, about 1 cup (125 g)
1 cup (30 g) baby spinach
1 peeled lemon
½ inch (1 cm) of fresh gingerroot
10 mint leaves
1 cup (235 ml) cold coconut water
½ cup (120 ml) crushed ice
5 drops of liquid stevia or ½ tablespoon (10 g) honey or agave (optional)

1. Add the cucumber, apple, spinach, lemon, ginger, mint, coconut water, and ice to your blender container.

2. Blend until smooth and fully combined. Taste and see if you'd like additional sweetener. Add if desired, blending once more.

3. If you'd like a very smooth, pulp-free juice, strain the mixture over a medium-size bowl through a nut milk bag or fine-mesh strainer before serving. Serve immediately.

V GF DF NF LS

1 large pitted and peeled mango,
  about 1 cup (175 g)
½ of a chopped cucumber, about ½ cup
  (70 g)
1 small lime, peeled and halved
½ cup (120 ml) cold water
¼ cup (60 ml) crushed ice
5 drops of liquid stevia extract

1. Add the mango, cucumber, lime, water, ice, and stevia extract to your blender container.

2. Blend on high until smooth and fully combined.

3. If you'd like a very smooth, pulp-free juice, strain the mixture over a medium-size bowl through a nut milk bag or fine-mesh strainer before serving. Serve immediately.

▲ Mango Lime Cooler Juice

Makes 12 to 16 ounces (355 to 475 ml)

Something about this drink reminds me of the spa. Maybe it's the refreshing cucumber and lime, or maybe it's the exotic mango. Either way, this is sure to be on your "must make often" drink list. It's thick, naturally sweet, and extremely satisfying.

☞ RECIPE TIP

If you want to change up the flavor of your drink, try replacing any water in the recipe with coconut water. It has added electrolytes plus vitamins and adds a tropical flair.

Grapefruit Quencher Juice

Makes 12 to 16 ounces (355 to 475 ml)

Grapefruit may help with weight loss by helping to curb appetite, stimulating the metabolism, and reducing water weight. This very juicy grapefruit blend tastes fabulous with the addition of a sweet orange.

V **GF** **DF** **NF** **LS**

1 large grapefruit, peeled and quartered
1 orange, peeled and halved
½ cup (120 ml) cold coconut water
5 drops of liquid stevia extract
¼ cup (60 ml) crushed ice
1 tablespoon (20 g) honey or agave
  (optional)
Ice cubes for serving

1. Add the grapefruit, orange, coconut water, stevia extract, and ice to your blender container.

2. Blend on high until smooth and fully combined. Taste and see if you'd like additional sweetener. Add if desired, blending once more.

3. If you'd like a very smooth, pulp-free juice, strain the mixture over a medium-size bowl through a nut milk bag or fine-mesh strainer before serving. Serve immediately over ice, if desired.

Mint Fever Juice

Makes 12 to 16 ounces (355 to 475 ml)

Mint takes the front seat in this cooling and fresh green blend. If you don't have arugula or despise the taste, substitute with baby spinach in its place.

1 cup (150 g) green grapes
½ of chopped cucumber, about ½ cup (70 g)
1 cup (20 g) arugula
2 tablespoons (12 g) chopped fresh mint
1 cup (235 ml) cold coconut water
¼ cup (60 ml) crushed ice
5 drops of liquid stevia or ½ tablespoon (10 g) honey or agave (optional)

1. Add the green grapes, cucumber, arugula, mint, coconut water, and ice to your blender container.

2. Blend on high until smooth and the greens are fully combined. Taste and see if you'd like sweetener. Add if desired, blending once more.

3. If you'd like a very smooth, pulp-free juice, strain the mixture over a medium-size bowl through a nut milk bag or fine-mesh strainer before serving. Serve immediately.

Honeydew Limeade Juice

Makes 12 to 16 ounces (355 to 475 ml)

This very liquidy juice is cooling and refreshing at the same time. It's perfect for hydration on the days where you want a blissfully thirst-quenching blend.

1 cup (170 g) chopped honeydew melon, rind removed
1 lime, peeled and halved
½ cup (120 ml) cold coconut water
½ cup (120 ml) crushed ice
5 drops of liquid stevia or ½ tablespoon (10 g) honey or agave (optional)
Ice cubes for serving

1. Add the honeydew, lime, coconut water, and ice to your blender container.

2. Blend on high until smooth and fully combined. Taste and see if you'd like additional sweetener. Add if desired, blending once more.

3. If you'd like a very smooth, pulp-free juice, strain the mixture over a medium-size bowl through a nut milk bag or fine-mesh strainer before serving. Serve immediately over ice, if desired.

Make juice and smoothie bags at the beginning of each week to save on time. Simply put the premeasured ingredients in a plastic bag and store it in the refrigerator for later use. When it's time to make your juice, just toss the produce plus the liquid into the blender and blend. If you'd like to make premeasured bags to store in the freezer, that works too, but you'll need more liquid for blending than the recipe calls for.

Cranberry Crush Juice

Makes 12 to 16 ounces (355 to 475 ml)

Cranberries are naturally sour, but the apple, grapes, and coconut water help reduce that in this incredibly cleansing drink that may help with overall urinary tract health.

1 cored and chopped red apple, about 1 cup (125 g)
½ cup (50 g) fresh cranberries
¼ cup (38 g) green grapes
½ cup (120 ml) cold coconut water
¼ cup (60 ml) crushed ice
4 drops of liquid stevia extract
1 tablespoon (20 g) honey or agave (optional)

1. Add the apple, cranberries, green grapes, coconut water, ice, and stevia extract to your blender container.

2. Blend on high until smooth and fully combined. Taste and see if you'd like additional sweetener. Add if desired, blending once more.

3. If you'd like a very smooth, pulp-free juice, strain the mixture over a medium-size bowl through a nut milk bag or fine-mesh strainer before serving. Serve immediately.

Grape Starlet Juice

Makes 12 to 16 ounces (355 to 475 ml)

Sweet and fresh, this amped-up grape juice will hydrate and cleanse. If you want to go green, add in 1 cup (30 g) of spinach to the ingredient list to up your leafy green intake for the day.

V **GF** **DF** **NF** **LS**

1 cup (150 g) green grapes
1 chopped celery stalk, about ¼ cup (25 g)
½ of a chopped cucumber, about ½ cup (70 g)
½ cup (120 ml) cold coconut water
¼ cup (60 ml) crushed ice
5 drops of liquid stevia or ½ tablespoon (10 g) honey or agave (optional)

1. Add the green grapes, celery, cucumber, coconut water, and ice to your blender container.

2. Blend on high until smooth and fully combined. Taste and see if you'd like additional sweetener. Add if desired, blending once more.

3. If you'd like a very smooth, pulp-free juice, strain the mixture over a medium-size bowl through a nut milk bag or fine-mesh strainer before serving. Serve immediately.

☞ BLENDING TIP

For the juiciest blender juice, it's best to use fresh fruit for whole food juices and not frozen fruit. Frozen fruit works best in smoothies where you crave a thicker, denser consistency.

Green Balancer Juice

Makes 12 to 16 ounces (355 to 475 ml)

This juice is a powerhouse of all the best fruits and veggies to fight excess bloat and inflammation. It also aids in alkalizing the body. It's a perfect way to start your day or to end it, and this green drink may help balance and restore your system.

V **GF** **DF** **NF** **LS**

1 cup (155 g) chopped pineapple, rind removed
¼ of a chopped cucumber, about ¼ cup (35 g)
1 chopped celery stalk, about ¼ cup (25 g)
½ cup (15 g) baby spinach
½ cup (34 g) baby kale
½ cup (120 ml) cold coconut water
¼ cup (60 ml) crushed ice
5 drops of liquid stevia or ½ tablespoon (10 g) honey or agave (optional)

1. Add the pineapple, cucumber, celery, spinach, kale, coconut water, and ice to your blender container.

2. Blend on high until smooth and the greens are fully combined. Taste and see if you'd like sweetener. Add if desired, blending once more.

3. If you'd like a very smooth, pulp-free juice, strain the mixture over a medium-size bowl through a nut milk bag or fine-mesh strainer before serving. Serve immediately.

Ginger Pear Paradise Juice

Makes 12 to 16 ounces (355 to 475 ml)

Ginger spikes the flavor in juices. It also hides veggies like spinach and zucchini. This blend is amazing for relieving constipation and gaining extra potassium.

1 cored and chopped pear, about 1 cup (161 g)
½ of a chopped zucchini, about ½ cup (60 g)
1 cup (30 g) baby spinach
½ inch (1 cm) of ginger, chopped
½ cup (120 ml) cold coconut water
¼ cup (60 ml) crushed ice
3 drops of liquid stevia extract
½ tablespoon (10 g) honey or agave (optional)

1. Add the pear, zucchini, spinach, ginger, coconut water, ice, and stevia extract to your blender container.

2. Blend on high until smooth and fully combined. Taste and see if you'd like additional sweetener. Add if desired, blending once more.

3. If you'd like a very smooth, pulp-free juice, strain the mixture over a medium-size bowl through a nut milk bag or fine-mesh strainer before serving. Serve immediately.

Red Sweetie Juice

Makes 12 to 16 ounces (355 to 475 ml)

Red fruits and veggies make their debut in this sweet and simple combination. Full of iron and antioxidants, your taste buds will be so happy this beautiful blend made it into your day.

½ of a chopped beet, about ½ cup (113 g)
1 small lemon, peeled and halved
½ cup (85 g) chopped strawberries
1 cup (235 ml) cold coconut water
¼ cup (60 ml) crushed ice
½ tablespoon (10 g) honey or agave

1. Put the beet, lemon, strawberries, coconut water, ice, and honey or agave in your blender container.

2. Blend on high until smooth and the beet has fully combined. Taste and add more sweetener, if you'd like.

3. If you'd like a very smooth, pulp-free juice, strain the mixture over a medium-size bowl through a nut milk bag or fine-mesh strainer before serving. Serve immediately.

Green Grace Juice

Makes 20 to 25 ounces (560 to 700 ml)

You'll never know that the spinach is in this juice, except for the beautiful light green color that gives it away. It's not too sweet, and it's beautifully thick—a great combination for breakfast. I have a feeling you'll enjoy the subtle hint of vanilla. This recipe makes enough for 2 or 3, so share!

V **GF** **DF** **NF** **LS**

½ of a chopped cucumber, about ½ cup (70 g)
1 small apple, cored and chopped
1 small pear, cored and chopped
1 small lemon, peeled and chopped
½ cup (15 g) spinach
½ cup (120 ml) cold water
¼ cup (60 ml) crushed ice
5 drops of liquid stevia extract
¼ teaspoon vanilla extract
½ tablespoon (10 g) honey or agave (optional)

1. Add the cucumber, apple, pear, lemon, spinach, water, ice, stevia extract, and vanilla to your blender container.

2. Blend on high until smooth and fully combined. Taste and see if you'd like additional sweetener. Add if desired, blending once more.

3. If you'd like a very smooth, pulp-free juice, strain the mixture over a medium-size bowl through a nut milk bag or fine-mesh strainer before serving. Serve immediately.

☞ **RECIPE TIP**

Fruits are naturally sweet, and you'll rarely need additional help from sweeteners when making juices. If you're using more vegetables than fruit in your recipe, stevia extract helps to bring out the sweetness without adding sugar. It's calorie-free and sugar-free, so it won't spike your insulin. If you don't like the taste of stevia, try honey or agave to gently sweeten the drink. Try adding ½ tablespoon at a time until you reach your desired sweetness.

Simple Orange Juice

Makes 12 to 16 ounces (355 to 475 ml)

Who doesn't love a glass of classic orange juice? Because oranges are so juicy, they blend wonderfully. If you prefer a pulp-free OJ, strain it in a nut milk bag or fine-mesh strainer before serving. If you're looking to make it stand out, plain orange juice tastes great spiked with fresh gingerroot. Add ¼ inch (6 mm) of ginger and blend with the ingredients if you'd like to try it.

V GF DF NF LS

2 large oranges, peeled and chopped
½ cup (120 ml) cold water
¼ cup (60 ml) crushed ice
5 drops of liquid stevia or ½ tablespoon
  (10 g) honey or agave (optional)
Ice cubes for serving

1. Add the oranges, water, and ice to your blender container.

2. Blend on high until smooth and fully combined. Taste and see if you'd like additional sweetener. Add if desired, blending once more.

3. If you'd like a very smooth, pulp-free juice, strain the mixture over a medium-size bowl through a nut milk bag or fine-mesh strainer before serving. Serve immediately over ice, if desired.

Orange Carrot Juice

Makes 12 to 16 ounces (355 to 475 ml)

Carrots work best as part of a juice blend because they lack juiciness and have a lot of fiber. No worries, though, because when combined with oranges, the blend is quenching, a powerhouse of nutrition, and a great way to get in your daily vitamin A and vitamin C.

V GF DF NF LS

2 oranges, peeled and chopped
1 chopped carrot, about ½ cup (65 g)
½ cup (120 ml) cold water
¼ cup (60 ml) crushed ice
5 drops of liquid stevia or ½ tablespoon
  (10 g) honey or agave (optional)
Ice cubes for serving

1. Add the oranges, carrot, water, and ice to your blender container.

2. Blend on high until smooth and fully combined. Taste and see if you'd like additional sweetener. Add if desired, blending once more.

3. If you'd like a very smooth, pulp-free juice, strain the mixture over a medium-size bowl through a nut milk bag or fine-mesh strainer before serving. Serve immediately over ice, if desired.

Red Apple Juice

Makes 12 to 16 ounces (355 to 475 ml)

Most people think that a blended apple would be extra sweet, but it's not. A little help from honey or stevia can sweeten up the drink a bit, so experiment with your taste buds by testing out which apples or sweeteners you like to make your perfect juice. My favorites are Granny Smith, Gala, and Pink Lady varieties. Blended apple juice is thick, so if you like the very juicy consistency of store-bought or juicer-made juice, you'll want to strain this mixture with a nut milk bag or fine-mesh strainer. This is one the kids and adults will love.

V **GF** **DF** **NF**

2 medium red apples, cored and chopped
1 cup (235 ml) cold water
½ cup (120 ml) crushed ice
1 tablespoon (20 g) honey
Additional sweeteners (optional)
Ice cubes for serving

1. Add the apples, water, ice, and honey to your blender container.

2. Blend on high until smooth and the peels are fully combined. Taste and see if you'd like additional sweetener. Add if desired, blending once more.

3. If you'd like a very smooth, pulp-free juice, strain the mixture over a medium-size bowl through a nut milk bag or fine-mesh strainer before serving. Serve immediately over ice, if desired.

☞ **BLENDING TIP**

While chopping produce for juices is necessary to get the recipe right, the blender can handle large pieces of fruit and vegetables when blending. Once you get the hang of making your own, you won't have to chop so finely when making the recipe. Blended juice recipes are very forgiving.

2

SMOOTHIES, SHAKES, AND
SLUSHIES

Smoothies are quite possibly the best drink in the world. Creamy, thick shakes can quench your thirst, replace a meal, or masquerade as a dessert—all while being healthy at the same time. Smoothies are a great way to incorporate greens and other juice boosters, such as chia, herbal vitamin powders, turmeric, and maca, that are otherwise hard to get into a healthy diet. These clean and nutritious shakes are a great way to start or end your day. Grab a bendy straw and let these special blends rock your taste buds!

Maca Mango Paradise Smoothie

Makes 12 to 16 ounces (355 to 475 ml)

Maca is known for its hormone-balancing and energizing properties. If you have frozen mango and pineapple chunks ready to go in your freezer, this simple recipe will put you in paradise. Adding cayenne pepper to this blend adds some heat and may help with improved circulation and metabolism.

(V) (GF) (DF) (NF) (LS)

1 cup (235 ml) cold coconut water
1 cup (30 g) spinach
1 cup (175 g) frozen chopped mango
½ cup (80 g) frozen chopped pineapple
  chunks
1 teaspoon maca powder
⅛ teaspoon cayenne pepper (optional)

1. Add the coconut water, spinach, mango, pineapple, maca, and cayenne pepper (if using) to your blender container.

2. Blend until smooth and combined, adding more liquid if necessary to blend. Serve immediately.

☞ **TIME-SAVING TIP**

To save on the time it takes to make smoothies, make smoothie bags by combining chopped fruit and greens inside preportioned plastic bags to store in the freezer.

Green Bliss Smoothie

Makes 12 to 16 ounces (355 to 475 ml)

Avocado seems like the strangest ingredient in this smoothie, but it makes this blend creamy, sweet, and full of healthy fat. It will be your new favorite for a filling breakfast or healthy meal replacement.

(V) (GF) (DF) (NF)

1 cup (235 ml) cold water
¼ cup (58 g) mashed avocado
1 cored and chopped small pear
1 cup (30 g) spinach
1 small lime, peeled and halved
1 or 2 pitted medjool dates
½ cup (120 ml) crushed ice

1. Add the water, avocado, pear, spinach, lime, 1 date, and ice to your blender container.

2. Blend until smooth and fully combined. Taste and add another date if you'd like more sweetness. Serve immediately.

Green Goddess Smoothie ▶

Makes 12 to 16 ounces (355 to 475 ml)

This is one of my all-time favorite smoothies, and it's one I made for years as my breakfast before walking into my office job. It's an easy go-to any time of day and a great supplement for replacing electrolytes after a hard workout. To really make this stand out, add spirulina to the ingredients for its cleansing and healing properties.

½ cup (120 ml) cold almond milk
1 peeled banana, broken in chunks
1 cup (30 g) fresh spinach
½ teaspoon vanilla extract
½ cup (120 ml) crushed ice
1 tablespoon (20 g) honey (omit for low-
  sugar option) or 1 pitted medjool date or
  5 drops of liquid stevia extract
½ teaspoon spirulina powder (optional)

1. Add the almond milk, banana, spinach, vanilla, ice, and sweetener to your blender container.

2. Blend on high until smooth or until the spinach has fully combined. Serve immediately.

☞ **NUTRITION TIP**

It's best to use ripe, brown spotted bananas for your smoothies. If the bananas are not ripe, they can cause belly bloating.

Kiwi Colada Smoothie

Makes 12 to 16 ounces (355 to 475 ml)

This is a true taste of the tropics, and it's a great way to use extra fresh pineapple and kiwi you might have in the summer months. It tastes absolutely divine on a hot, sunny day. To make this green, add 1 cup (30 g) of fresh spinach to the mix.

(V) (GF) (DF) (NF)

½ cup (120 ml) canned light coconut milk
½ cup (120 ml) cold water
1 tablespoon (15 ml) fresh lime juice
1 cup (155 g) chopped pineapple, rind removed
1 peeled and chopped kiwi
1 tablespoon (20 g) honey or agave
¼ cup (60 ml) crushed ice

1. Add the coconut milk, water, lime juice, pineapple, kiwi, honey or agave, and ice to your blender container.

2. Blend on high until smooth and fully combined. Serve immediately.

VARIATION: If you love essential oils, add one drop of lime or lemon essential oil to the ingredients before blending to enhance the flavor and add nutritional benefits.

☞ SMOOTHIE TIP

If you're concerned with sugar content but like a sweeter drink, omit any dates and honey. Use plain or flavored stevia drops to amp up the sweetness.

Strawberry Banana Smoothie

Makes 12 to 16 ounces (355 to 475 ml)

Before smoothies were cool, my mom would make me a smoothie just like this when I was a kid. The classic flavors of strawberry and banana go together so well. This is a great go-to blend when you're short on time, and it always tastes amazing.

(GF)

½ cup (120 ml) cold almond milk
½ cup (115 g) plain nonfat probiotic yogurt
1 peeled banana, broken apart in chunks
½ cup (85 g) chopped strawberries
1 tablespoon (20 g) honey or agave

1. Add the almond milk, yogurt, banana, strawberries, and honey or agave to your blender container.

2. Blend on high until smooth and fully combined. Serve immediately.

Sugar Cookie Smoothie ▶

Makes 16 to 20 ounces (475 to 570 ml)

If you love cashews, you'll love how perfect they taste in this smoothie that is reminiscent of a sweet sugar cookie. To make it even more nutritious and turn this into a green smoothie, add 1 cup (30 g) of spinach to the mix.

GF

1 cup (235 ml) almond milk
⅓ cup (77 g) plain probiotic yogurt
¼ cup (33 g) raw cashews
1 peeled banana, broken into chunks
½ tablespoon (10 g) honey or agave
1 pitted medjool date
½ teaspoon vanilla extract
½ cup (120 ml) crushed ice

1. Add the almond milk, yogurt, cashews, banana, honey or agave, date, vanilla, and ice to your blender container.

2. Blend on high until smooth and fully combined. Serve immediately.

☞ **BLENDING TIP**

Smoothies taste even better when you use a homemade, preservative-free milk, found in chapter 4. Make a batch of one of these milks each week for easy smoothie making.

Cinnamon Orange Sunrise Smoothie

Makes 12 to 16 ounces (355 to 475 ml)

Oranges and bananas are the best combination, especially for breakfast. Here, I've paired it with turmeric and cinnamon to make it a super anti-inflammatory blend.

½ cup (120 ml) rice milk
1 medium orange, peeled and chopped
1 peeled banana, broken into chunks
½ teaspoon vanilla extract
¼ teaspoon ground turmeric
½ teaspoon ground cinnamon
½ cup (120 ml) crushed ice
½ tablespoon (10 g) honey or agave

1. Add the rice milk, orange, banana, vanilla, turmeric, cinnamon, ice, and honey or agave to your blender container.

2. Blend on high until smooth and fully combined. Serve immediately.

Strawberry Shortcake Smoothie

Makes 16 to 20 ounces (475 to 570 ml)

Strawberry shortcake in a glass? Yes, please! You'll be putting this dessert-like blend on your make-all-the-time list. Bonus: you'll never suspect it has spinach and beets in it.

1 cup (235 ml) rice milk
½ cup (85 g) chopped strawberries
1 small chopped raw beet, about 1 cup (225 g)
1 cup (30 g) spinach
1 small cored and chopped apple, about ½ cup (63 g)
1 tablespoon (20 g) honey or agave
1 pitted medjool date
½ cup (120 ml) crushed ice

1. Add the rice milk, strawberries, beet, spinach, apple, honey or agave, date, and ice to your blender container.

2. Blend on high until smooth and fully combined. Serve immediately.

Cherry Pecan Pie Smoothie

Makes 16 to 20 ounces (475 to 570 ml)

This easy smoothie tastes just like cherry pie in a glass. It's creamy, sweet, and nutty all in the same sip. Cherries help to remove uric acid buildup in your body, so if you have a condition like gout, you might like this as a preventative drink. I like to use sweet, dark, frozen cherries, but any variety will do.

V **GF** **DF**

1 cup (235 ml) water
1 peeled banana, broken into chunks
1 cup (155 g) frozen cherries
1 cup (67 g) kale
5 raw pecans
1 tablespoon (20 g) honey or agave

1. Add the water, banana, cherries, kale, pecans, and honey or agave to your blender container.

2. Blend on high until smooth and fully blended. Serve immediately.

 **BLENDING TIP**

Spinach and kale are the most used greens for smoothies, but almost all greens blend well. Try these recipes by experimenting with your favorite offbeat green that you may see at the farmer's market or that you have growing in your garden. It's a great way to rotate the greens you consume in your diet.

Ginger Orange Crush Smoothie

Makes 16 to 20 ounces (475 to 570 ml)

Ginger really spices up this orange smoothie into a drink you'll find yourself coming back to again and again. Not only does it taste great, the benefits of ginger are too good to be missed.

V **GF** **DF** **NF** **LS**

1 cup (235 ml) coconut milk
1 large orange, peeled and halved
1 large pear, cored and chopped
1 inch (2.5 cm) of peeled fresh ginger
½ cup (120 ml) crushed ice

1. Add the coconut milk, orange, pear, ginger, and ice to your blender container.

2. Blend on high until smooth and fully combined. Serve immediately.

Superfood Starlet Smoothie ▶

Makes 16 to 20 ounces (475 to 570 ml)

This superfood mix will fuel your energy for the day ahead, plus give you a load of nutrition. There's no need to get flaxmeal for this recipe—whole flaxseeds will blend nicely in your power blender.

1½ cups (120 ml) light coconut milk
1 cup (175 g) frozen chopped mango
1 cup (30 g) spinach
1 tablespoon (12 g) flaxseeds
1 tablespoon (15 g) bee pollen
1 teaspoon chia seeds
2 tablespoons (40 g) honey

1. Add the coconut milk, mango, spinach, flaxseeds, bee pollen, chia seeds, and honey to your blender container.

2. Blend on high until smooth and the flaxseeds have fully combined. Serve immediately.

☞ TIP

Smoothies with chia seeds don't usually keep well because they form a gelatin-like mixture after settling in liquid a few minutes. If you're adding in chia seeds to improve the health benefits of your smoothie, plan on consuming the smoothie immediately after it's made for the best texture.

1 cup (235 ml) almond milk
1 cup (150 g) red grapes, stems removed
1 peeled banana, broken into chunks
1 cup (30 g) spinach
2 tablespoons (32 g) peanut butter
½ cup (120 ml) crushed ice

1. Add the almond milk, red grapes, banana, spinach, peanut butter, and ice to your blender container.

2. Blend on high until smooth and fully combined. Serve immediately.

Orange Dream Pop Smoothie

Makes 16 to 20 ounces (475 to 570 ml)

Warning! This one's addictive. It tastes just like the orange-and-cream popsicles we ate as kids. Get excited to try this healthified version. If you love the flavor and think it would be great as a popsicle, you're right! Pour this mixture into popsicle molds and freeze them overnight for dessert the next day.

▲ Peanut Butter and Jam Smoothie

Makes 16 to 20 ounces (475 to 570 ml)

A green smoothie that tastes like PB and J? Oh yes, you've found it! You're going to love this healthy combo that tastes just like your favorite childhood sandwich. If you want to up your leafy green game, add an additional 1 cup (30 g) of spinach to this mix—you won't taste it.

¼ cup (60 ml) rice milk
½ cup (115 g) plain probiotic yogurt
1 peeled banana, broken into chunks
1 large orange, peeled and chopped
½ teaspoon orange zest
½ teaspoon vanilla extract
1 tablespoon (20 g) honey or agave
½ cup (120 ml) crushed ice

1. Add the rice milk, yogurt, banana, orange, orange zest, vanilla, honey or agave, and ice to your blender container.

2. Blend on high until smooth and fully combined. Serve immediately.

VARIATION: If you love essential oils, add one drop of orange essential oil to the ingredients before blending to enhance the flavor and add nutritional benefits.

Parsley Power Smoothie

Makes 12 to 16 ounces (355 to 475 ml)

Parsley is extremely good for heavy metal detox, and you'll never detect it in this recipe. You might also find it gives you some great energy for the day ahead. This recipe is surprisingly fresh and light.

½ cup (120 ml) cold water
½ cup (15 g) fresh parsley
1 small peeled banana, broken into chunks
1 small apple, cored and chopped
1 pitted medjool date
½ cup (120 ml) crushed ice

1. Add the water, parsley, banana, apple, date, and ice to your blender container.

2. Blend on high until smooth and fully blended. Serve immediately.

☞ **BLENDING TIP**

If you have insulin problems or are concerned with sugar in your diet, add a healthy fat into your blend. Healthy fats, such as coconut oil or fresh avocado, when mixed with sugary fruits in a smoothie will help the sugar to digest more slowly into your bloodstream.

☞ **TIME-SAVING TIP**

Make your smoothies ahead of time and store them in an airtight glass container for up to 3 days. When you're ready to consume it, the blend will be ready for you. Some blends won't taste as good as freshly made, but do help save on time.

Coco Green Cantaloupe Smoothie

Makes 16 to 20 ounces (475 to 570 ml)

If you're a cantaloupe lover, try this decadent coconut version. You'll love the texture that the coconut flakes give it, and you'll get your greens in, too. If you don't have cantaloupe on hand, fresh papaya is a good substitute.

½ cup (120 ml) canned light coconut milk
2 cups (320 g) chopped cantaloupe, rind removed
1 cup (30 g) spinach
2 tablespoons (8 g) unsweetened coconut flakes
1 tablespoon (20 g) honey or agave
½ cup (120 ml) crushed ice

1. Add the coconut milk, cantaloupe, spinach, coconut flakes, honey or agave, and ice to your blender container.

2. Blend on high until smooth and fully combined. Serve immediately.

High Energy Mix Smoothie

Makes 16 to 20 ounces (475 to 570 ml)

This is one amazing smoothie. It's full of nutrients and flavor, and the ingredients mix together so well. Once I start drinking it, I can't stop. If you love them, adding in 2 tablespoons (20 g) of dried goji berries makes this a standout blend.

1 cup (235 ml) hemp milk
2 tablespoons (30 g) tahini
5 chopped strawberries, about ¾ cup (128 g)
1 peeled banana, broken into chunks
1 cup (30 g) spinach
1 teaspoon cinnamon
1 tablespoon (20 g) honey or agave
½ cup (120 ml) crushed ice

1. Add the hemp milk, tahini, strawberries, banana, spinach, cinnamon, honey or agave, and ice to your blender container.

2. Blend on high until smooth and fully combined. Serve immediately.

Mint Chocolate Chip Smoothie ▶

Makes 16 to 20 ounces (475 to 570 ml)

This smoothie tastes just like ice cream, but better! Nothing is more awesome than the heavenly, candied flavor of mint + chocolate. Bonus: this is naturally green-hued from the kale and spinach.

GF **NF**

½ cup (120 ml) canned light coconut milk
½ cup (115 g) plain probiotic yogurt
1 peeled banana, broken into chunks
1 cup (30 g) spinach
1 cup (67 g) kale
½ teaspoon vanilla extract
1 teaspoon mint extract
3 tablespoons (33 g) chopped dark chocolate or chocolate chips
2 tablespoons (40 g) honey or agave
½ cup (120 ml) crushed ice, plus more if needed
Chocolate shavings or additional chocolate chips for serving

1. Add the coconut milk, yogurt, banana, spinach, kale, vanilla, mint extract, chocolate chips, honey or agave, and ice to your blender container.

2. Blend on high until smooth and fully combined, at least 25 seconds. This smoothie tastes better when it's thick, so you might need to add more ice.

3. Pour into a glass and add chocolate shavings or chips on top. Serve immediately.

☞ **BLENDING TIP**

Most smoothies taste best when you blend them with ice. It helps the texture and the taste. If you prefer to not use ice but like the frozen element, you can always slice and freeze fruit to be used in your recipe ahead of time. Frozen fruit will create the same effect as ice.

Berry Oat Breakfast Shake ▶

Makes 16 to 20 ounces (475 to 570 ml)

Oats have an awesome amount of fiber and help sweep out toxins and cholesterol from your body. Including them in a smoothie is a great way to gain these benefits. The thick texture oats add also really compliments the drink. It's absolutely perfect for breakfast time. Make this dairy-free by using coconut yogurt in place of the probiotic yogurt.

GF

1 cup (235 ml) almond milk
½ cup (115 g) plain probiotic yogurt
1 peeled banana, broken into chunks
½ cup (weight will vary) frozen mixed berries
¼ cup (24 g) gluten-free old-fashioned rolled oats
1 tablespoon (20 g) maple syrup

1. Add the almond milk, yogurt, banana, mixed berries, rolled oats, and maple syrup to your blender container.

2. Blend on high until smooth and fully combined. Serve immediately.

Antioxidant Balancer Smoothie

Makes 16 to 20 ounces (475 to 570 ml)

This antioxidant-spiked drink will surprise you. You'll taste sweet berries and pineapple—and you'll never taste the broccoli. That makes it a perfect way to get the kids to consume this green vegetable. If you like ginger, throw in a little sliver—it enhances the flavors in this blend.

GF **NF**

½ cup (120 ml) cold water
½ cup (75 g) blueberries
1 cup (155 g) chopped pineapple, rind
 removed
1 cup (156 g) frozen broccoli
¼ cup (60 g) plain probiotic yogurt
1 tablespoon (20 g) honey or agave, plus
 more to taste

1. Add the water, blueberries, pineapple, broccoli, yogurt, and honey or agave to your blender container.

2. Blend on high until smooth and fully combined. Taste and add more sweetener if desired. Serve immediately.

Green Fuel Protein Shake

Makes 16 to 20 ounces (475 to 570 ml)

If you're looking for the perfect way to incorporate your favorite protein powder into a simple post-workout smoothie, use this recipe. It turns out great every time. My favorite feature of this drink is that it's thick and milkshake-like. If you like this mix, freeze several peeled bananas; ahead of time so you can make this a quick blend after a workout. You can use fresh bananas, you'll just need to add ice. To up the nutrition content, add 1 tablespoon (9 g) of raw shelled hemp seeds to the ingredients.

V **GF** **DF** **NF**

1 cup (235 ml) hemp milk, plus more to
 taste
1 frozen banana, peeled and chopped,
 about 1 cup (150 g)
1 cup (67 g) kale
2 tablespoons (10 g) protein powder,
 any flavor
1 pitted medjool date

1. Add the hemp milk, banana, kale, protein powder, and date to your blender container.

2. Blend on high until smooth and fully combined, adding more liquid if desired. Serve immediately.

☞ **BLENDING TIP**

Greens with hard stems need de-stemming before blending in a regular blender, but they will blend well *with* their stems in high-powered blenders. Feel free to use those stems you might otherwise throw away.

Chocolate Silk Shake

Makes 16 to 20 ounces (475 to 570 ml)

If you like chocolate shakes, here's a healthified version for you. You'll never taste the greens, and believe me when I say that you'll want to have this every day—for dessert. If you like coffee and chocolate mixes, add 1 teaspoon of instant espresso powder to this blend for a richer flavor.

1 cup (235 ml) almond milk
1 peeled banana, broken into chunks
2 tablespoons (32 g) almond butter
1 tablespoon (5 g) cocoa powder
2 tablespoons (40 g) maple syrup
1 cup (30 g) spinach
1 cup (235 ml) crushed ice

1. Add the almond milk, banana, almond butter, cocoa powder, maple syrup, spinach, and ice to your blender container.

2. Blend until smooth and fully combined. Add more ice if you want a thicker shake. Serve immediately.

Sugar-Free Green Shake

Makes 12 to 16 ounces (355 to 475 ml)

If you want a truly low-sugar green smoothie, this mix is the way to go. Stevia extract plus strawberry extract combine with high-antioxidant berries and lemon to sweeten up the blend without spiking your insulin. This also tastes great with other fruit extracts, so experiment with flavors to make the perfect mix.

½ cup (120 ml) water
2 cups (134 g) kale
½ cup (75 g) blueberries
2 chopped strawberries
½ teaspoon liquid stevia extract
½ teaspoon strawberry extract
½ of a large peeled lemon
½ cup (120 ml) crushed ice

1. Add the water, kale, blueberries, strawberries, stevia extract, strawberry extract, lemon, and ice to your blender container.

2. Blend until smooth and fully combined, at least 30 seconds. Serve immediately.

Vanilla Oat Protein Shake

Makes 16 to 20 ounces (475 to 570 ml)

This fail-safe protein shake is a great way to use your favorite protein powder. If you have additional greens or fruit lying around, you can throw it in to switch up the flavor and nutrition profile. To make this even healthier, add 1 tablespoon (5 g) of crushed raw walnuts to the blend (omit for nut-free option).

GF **NF**

½ cup (120 ml) oat milk
½ cup (115 g) plain probiotic yogurt
¼ cup (20 g) vanilla protein powder
1 teaspoon vanilla extract
1 tablespoon (20 g) honey or agave
1 cup (235 ml) crushed ice, plus more
  if needed

1. Add the oat milk, yogurt, protein powder, vanilla, honey or agave, and ice to your blender container.

2. Blend on high until smooth and fully combined. Add more ice if you'd like a thicker shake. Serve immediately.

Dairy-Free Strawberry Milkshake

Makes 12 to 16 ounces (355 to 475 ml)

I love strawberries and strawberry ice cream treats. This tastes just like you blended up sugary sweet strawberries with ice cream, but it's a whole lot healthier. Full-fat coconut milk is key in this recipe to make it rich and creamy just like half-and-half would.

V **GF** **DF** **NF**

1 cup (235 ml) full-fat canned coconut milk
½ teaspoon vanilla extract
2 tablespoons (40 g) honey or agave
1 cup (170 g) frozen chopped strawberries

1. Add the coconut milk, vanilla, honey or agave, and strawberries, in that order, to your blender container.

2. Pulse to get the mixture moving and then blend on high. Blend until smooth and combined, using your tamper if needed. Add more liquid, if necessary, to reach your desired consistency. Serve immediately.

Peach Milkshake

Makes 12 to 16 ounces (355 to 475 ml)

Like a cross between peach pie and peach ice cream, this is the best frozen treat in the summer. Add a scoop of vanilla protein powder to it after a workout, and you'll be in heaven. This is indulgent with the half-and-half, but it's a great treat. Make this dairy-free by replacing the half-and-half with full-fat coconut milk.

GF **NF**

½ cup (120 ml) half-and-half
1 teaspoon vanilla extract
2 tablespoons (40 g) honey or agave
2 cups (500 g) chopped frozen peaches

1. Add the half-and-half, vanilla, honey or agave, and chopped peaches, in that order, to your blender container.

2. Pulse to get the mixture moving and then blend on high. Blend until smooth and combined, using your tamper if needed. Add more liquid, if necessary, to reach your desired consistency. Serve immediately.

Frozen Lemonade Slushie ▶

Makes 16 to 20 ounces (475 to 570 ml)

Last summer when on vacation with my family at the beach, we stopped by a coffee shop that served up delightful frozen lemonades to offer a break from the heat. I loved them, and I wanted to re-create it for myself. I think you'll like it, too. I've found that stevia extract enhances fresh lemons beautifully and reduces the sugar in drinks like these that need to have sweetness for a refreshing taste. Coconut water amps up your electrolytes and hydration.

V **GF** **DF** **NF**

1 cup (235 ml) cold coconut water
2 small lemons, peeled and halved
2 cups (475 ml) ice cubes
10 drops of liquid stevia extract
2 tablespoons (40 g) honey or agave

1. Add the coconut water, lemons, ice, stevia extract, and honey or agave to your blender container.

2. Blend on high until fully combined and smooth, but still icy. If you overblend, the machine will heat up and melt the mixture. Serve immediately.

Raspberry Green Tea Slushie

Makes about 2 cups (475 ml)

Slushies are a fun treat when it's hot out. This healthified version is divine and low in sugar. It's a perfect addition to an outdoor barbeque when you need a light palate cleanser after a heavy meal.

(V) (GF) (DF) (NF)

1 cup (235 ml) cold green tea
1½ cups (375 g) frozen red raspberries
5 drops of liquid stevia extract
1 teaspoon honey or agave

1. Add the green tea, raspberries, stevia extract, and honey or agave to your blender container.

2. Blend on high until fully combined and smooth, but still icy. If you overblend, the machine will heat up and melt the mixture. Pour into a tall glass and serve with a spoon. Serve immediately.

Watermelon Mint Slushie

Makes about 2 cups (475 ml)

Great for kids or adults, this sweet watermelon dessert is the best in the summer months when watermelon is ripe. Freeze watermelon cubes and have them ready because you'll have people begging to make this for them. Boost this slushie by adding 1 tablespoon (15 ml) of fresh aloe vera juice to the blend.

(V) (GF) (DF) (NF) (LS)

½ cup (120 ml) cold coconut water
2 cups (300 g) frozen chopped watermelon
2 tablespoons (12 g) chopped fresh mint

1. Add the coconut water, watermelon, and mint to your blender container.

2. Blend on high until fully combined and smooth, but still icy. If you overblend, the machine will heat up and melt the mixture. Pour into a tall glass and serve with a spoon. Serve immediately.

3

COFFEE DRINKS, MATCHA DRINKS, AND CREAMERS

If you're a java-lover, you'll be thrilled to know that your blender can help you out in this area, too. Make healthy homemade creamers for your daily cafe, creamy butter coffee, or blended frozen drinks for a midday pick-me-up. There's nothing better than indulging in your own homemade coffee drink that you can customize—all without leaving your house or breaking the bank.

Café Creme Butter Coffee

Makes 1 serving, 10 ounces (285 ml)

If you haven't tried butter coffee, it's time to get on the bandwagon. Butter coffee provides healthy fats that are healing for your body and fantastic for your brain.

GF **LS**

1 cup (235 ml) strong-brewed hot coffee
1 teaspoon vanilla extract
1 teaspoon coconut oil or MCT oil
1 teaspoon Cashew Creamer (page 71)
1 teaspoon unsalted grass-fed butter
1 teaspoon honey or maple syrup or
⅛ teaspoon liquid stevia (optional for sweetness)

1. Add the coffee, vanilla, coconut oil, Cashew Creamer, butter, and sweetener (if using) to your blender container.

2. Blend for a few seconds until fully combined and frothy. Serve immediately.

☞ BLENDING TIP

Most power blender containers will be able to handle hot liquids such as coffee and tea. Be sure to check your manufacturer's instructions if you aren't certain yours is made of a heatproof material to avoid any damage.

Matcha Latte

Makes 1 serving, 8 ounces (235 ml)

This lovely latte is made with matcha green tea powder and is a great alternative to other tea or coffee blends. Matcha is high in antioxidants and lower in caffeine than coffee. It also tastes fabulous! You can make this with light coconut milk, but I prefer the richer flavor of full-fat coconut milk.

½ cup (120 ml) full-fat coconut milk
½ cup (120 ml) water
1 teaspoon matcha powder
1 tablespoon (20 g) honey, maple syrup, or agave

1. Add the coconut milk, water, matcha powder, and sweetener to your blender container.

2. Blend on high until smooth and heated, about 1 to 2 minutes. Serve.

Coconut Creamer

Makes 2 cups (475 ml)

Coconut creamer is super easy to make if you have a can of full-fat coconut milk in your pantry. Unlike some nut-based creamers, there's no need to strain the mixture when you're done blending. While coconut imparts a slight tropical flavor, I find it's fabulous in coffee for the days when you want something different. It also combines well with flavored stevia drops to make many sugar-free coffee variations.

1 can (13.5 ounce, or 400 ml) full-fat coconut milk
1 tablespoon (15 ml) vanilla extract
1 tablespoon (20 g) honey or maple syrup, or 1 pitted date (optional for sweetness)

1. Place the coconut milk, vanilla, and sweetener (if using) in your blender container.

2. Blend until smooth and combined, adding more sweetener or vanilla to taste.

3. Store in a sealed glass jar in the refrigerator for up to 5 days.

Almond Creamer

Makes 2 cups (475 ml)

This classic is the most popular version of nut-based creamers on the market today—and for good reason. Almond creamer is extremely silky smooth and neutral tasting, so it works well in many recipes, not just coffee. If you want to use it in other preparations as a substitute for half-and-half or dairy creamer, leave out the sweetener.

V **GF** **DF** **LS**

1 cup (145 g) raw unroasted almonds
1½ cups (355 ml) water
1 tablespoon (15 ml) vanilla extract
1 tablespoon (20 g) honey or maple syrup,
   or 1 pitted date (optional)

1. Soak the almonds in a bowl of water for 8 hours or overnight. Once the nuts are hydrated and plump, dump the water, reserving the nuts.

2. Place the almonds, water, vanilla, and sweetener (if using) in your blender container. Blend on high until smooth and completely combined, at least 60 seconds. Add more sweetener, if desired, and blend to combine.

3. If you like a smooth creamer with no nut sediment in it, strain it through a nut milk bag, fine-mesh strainer, or cheesecloth before consuming.

4. Store in a sealed glass jar in the refrigerator for up to 5 days.

☞ SERVING TIP

If you choose to strain your almond creamer, you'll be left with delicious almond pulp. Make energy balls by mixing the pulp in a bowl with honey, chopped dried fruit, and unsweetened coconut flakes. Roll this mixture into balls and store them in the fridge for a quick and easy snack.

Cashew Creamer

Makes 2 cups (475 ml)

Cashew-based creamers are extremely rich and creamy—and this one is no exception. It mixes well in coffee and other coffee drinks. It's definitely the closest nondairy version of creamer I've found to half-and-half. I often prefer this to my almond creamer because it doesn't require straining after blending.

(V) (GF) (DF) (LS)

1 cup (140 g) raw, unroasted cashews
1½ cups (355 ml) filtered water
1 tablespoon (15 ml) vanilla extract
1 tablespoon (20 g) honey or maple syrup,
  or 1 pitted date (optional)

1. Soak the cashews in a bowl of water for 2 hours. Once the nuts are hydrated and plump, dump the water, reserving the nuts.

2. Place the cashews, water, vanilla, and sweetener (if using) in your blender. Blend on high until smooth and completely combined, at least 60 seconds. Add more sweetener, if desired, and blend to combine.

3. Store in a sealed glass jar in the refrigerator for up to 5 days.

☞ **BLENDING TIP**

If you don't have time to soak nuts for your nut-based creamers, you can still make the recipe, but it will require more water for blending and a longer blend time. It will not be as silky smooth—but no worries, it's still delicious!

4

NUT MILKS AND OTHER NONDAIRY MILKS

Homemade nondairy milks and nut milks are great alternatives to dairy milks. They are nutritious and taste heavenly. Flavor them to your liking and use them as you would in any recipe that calls for a milk. You'll find that plant-based milks work well in many of the recipes in this book and in your own. Try them in smoothies, soups, and sorbets. Once you make a few of your own homemade milk drinks, you'll never go back to store-bought again.

Macadamia Milk

Makes 3 cups (700 ml)

Macadamias are one of my favorite nuts. They have a smooth flavor and make a creamy, sweet milk. Many macadamia nuts are sold rancid, so try to find a fresh source.

1 cup (135 g) raw unroasted macadamia nuts
3 cups (700 ml) water
1 tablespoons (15 ml) vanilla extract
2 tablespoons (40 g) honey, maple syrup, or agave (optional)
1 tablespoon (14 g) coconut butter (optional)

1. Soak the macadamia nuts in a bowl of water for 2 hours. Once the nuts are hydrated and plump, dump the water and rinse the nuts.

2. Place the macadamia nuts, water, vanilla, sweetener (if using), and coconut butter (if using) in your blender container. Blend until smooth.

3. Macadamia milk is pretty smooth unstrained. If you like a smoother milk with no nut sediment in it, strain it through a nut milk bag, fine-mesh strainer, or cheesecloth before consuming.

Pistachio Milk

Makes 3 cups (700 ml)

Delicate and slightly nutty is how I'd describe this velvety pistachio milk. It's high in vitamin E, potassium, and vitamin K, so you'll love what it can do for your health, too.

1 cup (123 g) raw unroasted shelled pistachios
3 cups (700 ml) water
1 tablespoon (15 ml) vanilla extract
2 tablespoons (40 g) honey, maple syrup, or agave (optional for sweetness)
1 tablespoon (14 g) coconut butter (optional)

1. Soak the pistachios in water overnight or for 8 hours. Once the nuts are hydrated and plump, dump the water.

2. Place the pistachios, water, vanilla, sweetener (if using), and coconut butter (if using) in your blender container. Blend until smooth.

3. If you like a smoother milk with no nut sediment in it, strain it through a nut milk bag, fine-mesh strainer, or cheesecloth before consuming.

▲ Banana Milk

Makes 2 cups (475 ml)

You would assume banana milk tastes very banana-y. Surprisingly, it's not overwhelming. It's a smooth milk, fast to make, has a light flavor, and is a perfect substitute for dairy.

2 bananas, peeled and broken apart
1 cup (235 ml) water
1 tablespoon (15 ml) vanilla extract
2 tablespoons (40 g) honey, maple syrup, or agave (optional)

1. Place the bananas, water, vanilla, and sweetener (if using) in your blender container.

2. Blend until smooth. There's no need to strain this milk, either, as the blender whips it into the perfect milky texture.

THE RECIPES

PART 2:

THINGS TO EAT

5

JAMS, BUTTERS, AND SYRUPS

Healthy syrups, butters, and jams enhance your food in a unique way and can take your meals to another level. Making these just might be one of the most common, day-to-day uses of your power blender. Before you know it, you'll be adding Strawberry Chia Jam to your oatmeal, spreading homemade Honey Peanut Butter on celery sticks for a midday snack, and pouring Blueberry Fruit Syrup over your protein pancakes on Saturday mornings. Now, doesn't that sound fabulous! I think you'll find yourself making these classics often and even spicing them up to create your own versions.

▲ Strawberry Chia Jam

Makes 1⅓ cups (about 420 g)

This amazing blender jam uses no pectin or gelatin to set up; chia seeds do all the magic to naturally thicken the spread. It tastes wonderfully fresh and sweet— everything you'd expect from ripe summer strawberries.

 V   GF   DF   NF

¼ cup (120 ml) coconut water
4 pitted medjool dates
2 cups (340 g) fresh chopped strawberries, divided
2 tablespoons (26 g) chia seeds
10 drops of stevia glycerite

1. Add the coconut water and dates to your blender container. Blend on high for 30 to 60 seconds until the dates are broken up and almost smooth.

2. Add 1 cup (170 g) of strawberries and the chia seeds to the blender. Blend on low to gently mix it all together.

3. Add the remaining 1 cup (170 g) of strawberries and the stevia glycerite. Blend on low just until berries are broken up. You can make the jam as smooth or chunky as you'd like.

4. Pour into a small glass jar and chill in the refrigerator for a minimum of 30 minutes. The chia seeds will thicken the jam.

◄ Peach Apricot Jam

Makes 2 cups (about 640 g)

Smooth and sweet, this fruity jam can be used in nut butter sandwiches or spread on toast. You're just a few steps away from a quick and insanely tasty spread. There's no need to peel the peaches; the blender will chop right through them.

1 cup (250 g) fresh chopped peaches or thawed from frozen
½ cup (120 ml) water
¾ cup (98 g) dried unsweetened apricots, divided
1½ cups (300 g) sugar
2 tablespoons (28 ml) lemon juice
3 ounces (90 ml) liquid pectin

1. Add the peaches, water, ½ cup (65 g) of dried apricots, and sugar to your blender container.

2. Blend until very smooth. Add the lemon juice and pectin. Blend until combined.

3. Add the remaining ¼ cup (33 g) of apricots to the container. Pulse or blend on low until just combined, but still chunky, for texture. Let stand for 5 to 10 minutes.

4. Pour into glass jars, seal with a lid, and chill in the refrigerator for at least 8 hours. As the mixture cools and sits, it will thicken and change in color. Store in the refrigerator in an airtight glass or ceramic container.

Blueberry Chia Jam

Makes 1⅓ cups (about 400 g)

This jam is silky smooth and super fresh. It's good on toast, or try topping your ice cream or your Sunday morning pancakes with it.

¼ cup (60 ml) water
4 medjool dates, pitted
2 cups (290 g) fresh blueberries, divided
2 tablespoons (26 g) chia seeds
10 drops of stevia glycerite

1. Add the water and dates to your blender. Blend on high for 30 to 60 seconds until the dates are broken up and almost smooth.

2. Add 1 cup (145 g) of blueberries and the chia seeds to the blender. Blend on low to gently mix it all together.

3. Add the remaining 1 cup (145 g) of blueberries and the stevia glycerite. Pulse on low a few times just until berries are broken up. You can make the jam as smooth or chunky as you'd like.

4. Pour into a jar and chill in the refrigerator for a minimum of 30 minutes. The chia seeds will thicken the jam.

Raspberry Fruit Spread

Makes 1 cup (about 320 g)

Thick and rich, this healthified, naturally low-sugar spread can be made in minutes, and it is perfect for toast or anywhere fruit spread can enhance your dish. If you like a sweeter spread, add 1 tablespoon (20 g) of honey or 1 pitted date to the recipe until you reach your desired sweetness.

2 cups (250 g) fresh raspberries
½ cup (120 ml) water
2 tablespoons (28 ml) lemon juice
½ teaspoon liquid stevia glycerite
4 tablespoons (48 g) psyllium husk
¼ teaspoon vanilla extract

1. Add the raspberries, water, lemon juice, stevia glycerite, psyllium husk, and vanilla to your blender container.

2. Blend until smooth.

3. Store in the refrigerator in an airtight glass or ceramic container.

Classic Salted Butter

Makes 1 cup (225 g)

There is nothing like fresh, homemade butter, and your blender makes it super easy. Feel free to make flavored butters by adding spices or extracts at the end and blending for an additional few seconds. Making butter can take a few tries to master, but it is definitely worth the effort.

2 cups (475 ml) room temperature heavy cream
½ teaspoon pink Himalayan sea salt

1. Make sure the blender container is completely dry and all tools are cool. Place the heavy cream in your blender container.

2. Blend on a low to medium speed and then increase to high until the mixture is thicker. Stop to scrape down the sides. Blend again on medium speed for 5 seconds and stop to scrape down the sides. Repeat 2 to 3 times until solid butter sets up. Watch it carefully, as the blender can heat up and prevent the mixture from solidifying.

3. Place a fine-mesh strainer or nut milk bag over a bowl. Removing the butter from the blender container in batches, strain the butter through the strainer, pushing it through with a spatula to remove as much liquid as possible.

4. Add the sea salt to the butter and mix with a spatula.

5. Store in a glass mason jar or rolled in a parchment paper log that is tied at the ends.

Whipped Honey Butter

Makes 1 cup (225 g)

This butter is perfect on toast, breakfast bread, and muffins. It's rich, creamy, and sweet all at the same time.

8 tablespoons (112 g) unsalted butter, cut into chunks
¼ cup (60 ml) olive oil
¼ cup (85 g) honey

1. Place the butter, olive oil, and honey in your blender container.

2. Blend until smooth. Store in a glass mason jar or rolled in a parchment paper log that is tied at the ends.

Whipped Garlic Herb Butter

Makes ¾ cup (168 g)

This herb butter is amazing on top of a steak, chicken, or seafood. Or serve it on fresh bread. I always keep a roll of this in my refrigerator because there is always a use for it.

GF **NF** **LS**

¾ cup (165 g) unsalted butter, cut in chunks
2 tablespoons (28 ml) olive oil
1 tablespoon (1 g) dried chives
1 tablespoon (1 g) dried parsley
¼ teaspoon garlic powder
¼ teaspoon sea salt

1. Place the butter, olive oil, chives, parsley, garlic powder, and sea salt in your blender container.

2. Blend until smooth, using the tamper or stopping to scrape down the sides. Store in a glass mason jar or rolled in a parchment paper log that is tied at the ends.

Honey Maple Almond Butter

Makes 2 cups (450 g)

Almond butter is a great nut butter alternative if you're allergic to other nuts or avoid peanuts. I've found that when you add honey and maple syrup it tastes surprisingly like peanut butter. If you love peanut butter but would rather consume other nut butters, this one is for you.

GF **DF**

2 cups (290 g) raw or roasted almonds
¼ teaspoon sea salt
3 tablespoons (60 g) maple syrup
2 tablespoons (40 g) honey
1 tablespoon (14 g) coconut oil

1. Place the almonds, sea salt, maple syrup, honey, and coconut oil in your blender container.

2. Blend on high until it forms a smooth butter, using the tamper or stopping to scrape down the sides.

3. Store in the refrigerator in an airtight glass or ceramic container.

Tahini Butter

Makes 2 cups (about 450 g)

Tahini is highly underrated and one of my favorite butters to use in a variety of preparations. I use tahini to make dips and even mix it in my soups as an alternative to dairy to make them creamy. This is especially good in black bean soup. Traditionally, tahini lends the distinct nutty flavor to hummus recipes. It's full of vitamins and good fats. If you'd like, you can use raw sesame seeds, but I prefer the roasted version because they are less bitter.

V **GF** **DF** **NF** **LS**

2 cups (288 g) sesame seeds, raw or dry roasted
½ teaspoon sea salt
4 tablespoons (60 ml) mild olive oil (optional but recommended for creaminess)

1. Place the sesame seeds, sea salt, and olive oil (if using) in your blender container.

2. Blend until it is a smooth, thick consistency like nut butter. You might have to stop the blender and scrape down the sides or use your tamper, if you have one, to press the seeds into the blades.

3. Store in the refrigerator in an airtight glass or ceramic container.

Date Caramel Butter

Makes 1 cup (about 240 g)

Absolutely incredible and sinfully addictive, this vegan caramel butter is thick, creamy, and perfect for serving alongside apple slices for a midday snack or dessert. It also doubles as an amazing whipped frosting for cake.

V GF DF NF

⅓ cup (80 ml) water
15 pitted medjool dates
1 teaspoon vanilla extract
⅛ teaspoon sea salt
2 tablespoons (28 ml) coconut cream, taken from the top of a full-fat coconut milk can
1 teaspoon lemon juice

1. Add the water, dates, vanilla, sea salt, coconut cream, and lemon juice to your blender container.

2. Blend until a smooth puree is reached, stopping to scrape down the sides and using the tamper to push the dates into the blades.

3. Store in the refrigerator in an airtight glass or ceramic container.

Chocolate Hazelnut Spread

Makes 2 cups (520 g)

If you can believe it, this is better than the popular versions of the chocolate hazelnut spread you buy in the store. Use any kind of dark chocolate you prefer, dairy-free or with an extra high cocoa content. All options work well. Buttery soft and delightfully sweet, you'll love to spread it on your toast, apple slices, or celery sticks. You also might want to slather a thin layer on your pancakes, too.

GF **DF**

2 cups (270 g) hazelnuts
2 ounces (55 g) unsweetened dark
  chocolate, broken into small pieces
⅓ cup (115 g) honey
3 tablespoons (42 g) coconut oil
¼ cup (60 ml) canned full-fat unsweetened
  coconut milk

1. Place the hazelnuts, dark chocolate, honey, and coconut oil in your blender container.

2. Blend until it becomes a smooth, creamy sauce, stopping to scrape down the sides. Use a tamper if you have one to push the nuts into the blades.

3. Store in the refrigerator in an airtight glass or ceramic container.

VARIATION: If you'd like to roast your hazelnuts for a toasted hazelnut flavor, follow these steps prior to step 1 above.

1. Preheat the oven to 350°F (180°C, or gas mark 4).

2. Place the hazelnuts on a cookie sheet in a single layer. Bake in the oven for 10 minutes or until they are very lightly browned and toasted. Be careful to not over toast them.

3. Remove them from the oven and cool. If your hazelnuts came with the skins on them, rub them lightly with your fingertips to remove the skin.

Coconut Butter

Makes 2½ cups (552 g)

I find coconut butter completely addictive and use it many ways—from adding it to smoothies, to spreading it on toast, to making coconut dessert balls. It's one of my favorite condiments.

V **GF** **DF** **NF** **LS**

5 cups (300 g) unsweetened coconut flakes
2 tablespoons (28 g) coconut oil

1. Add the coconut flakes and coconut oil to your blender.

2. Blend slowly until combined and then blend on high until smooth, stopping the machine to scrape the sides. If your machine has a tamper, use it to help process the coconut to push it into the blades.

3. Store in the refrigerator in an airtight glass or ceramic container.

☞ **SERVING TIP**

Make a quick snack or dessert by stuffing coconut butter into pitted dates for a healthy sweet treat.

Cinnamon Apple Butter

Makes 1¼ cup (about 400 g)

I love a good fruit spread, and this thick, luscious version is so easy to make in your blender. Use this sweet butter on anything from a fresh baguette, topping ice cream, or adding a dollop to crackers with a slice of Cheddar cheese. It's divine. I use Red Delicious apples, but any variety will work.

(V) (GF) (DF) (NF)

2 large apples, peeled, cored, and chopped, about 3 cups (375 g)
¼ cup (60 ml) water
2 pitted medjool dates
1 tablespoon (15 ml) lemon juice
3 tablespoons (60 g) molasses
½ teaspoon ground cinnamon

1. First, cook the apples. Add the raw apples and ¼ cup (60 ml) of water to a small stockpot. Cook, uncovered, over medium-low heat until soft, about 8 to 10 minutes until the water has evaporated. When cooked through, add the apples into your blender container.

2. Add the dates, lemon juice, molasses, and cinnamon to your blender container.

3. Blend on low to initially combine and then blend on high until very smooth.

4. Store in the refrigerator in an airtight glass or ceramic container. As the butter cools in the refrigerator, it will thicken and be just right after about 8 hours or overnight. This mixture should result in a butter that has a thick spreadable consistency, but if you'd like it thicker, simmer the apple butter mixture in a small stockpot until any extra water is evaporated and you reach your desired consistency.

☞ **SERVING TIP**

Mix this spread with 2 chopped apples topped with 2 tablespoons (16 g) of homemade granola for a quick breakfast bowl that tastes like apple pie.

Strawberry Fruit Syrup

Makes 1½ cups (about 480 g)

This syrup is great on anything you might like syrup on, such as ice cream or pancakes. It is also wonderful for making flavored desserts. Feel free to substitute stevia for the honey or agave in this recipe to make it sugar-free.

2 cups (340 g) fresh strawberries, tops removed, chopped
2 tablespoons (40 g) honey or agave
¼ cup (60 ml) water
⅛ teaspoon chia seeds

1. Add the strawberries, honey or agave, water, and chia seeds to your blender container.

2. Blend until completely smooth. As the mixture sits, it will thicken.

3. Store in the refrigerator in an airtight glass or ceramic container.

Blueberry Fruit Syrup

Makes 1½ cups (about 480 g)

Fantastic for drizzling on just about anything, I love to use this to enhance cheesecakes, pancakes, and banana whips. I find that agave syrup works better in this blend than honey, but both result in a great homemade syrup.

2 cups (290 g) fresh blueberries
2 tablespoons (40 g) honey or agave
¼ cup (60 ml) water
⅛ teaspoon chia seeds

1. Add the blueberries, honey or agave, water, and chia seeds to your blender container.

2. Blend until completely smooth. As the mixture sits, it will thicken.

3. Store in the refrigerator in an airtight glass or ceramic container.

> ☞ **SERVING TIP**
> Drizzle this syrup over homemade crepes or add 1 to 2 tablespoons (20 to 40 g) to smoothies for a berry flavor.

6

GUACAMOLES, HUMMUSES, AND OTHER DIPS AND SPREADS

Dips and spreads are some of my favorite foods and best loved recipes to make in my blender. The high-speed blender gives you the power to create the perfect texture for dips and spreads—thick and chunky or smooth and creamy. You'll find they are versatile and can easily enhance your sandwiches, toast, wraps, and even salads. Not to mention, you can create great snacks at a moment's notice or whip up amazing party-perfect appetizers.

◁ Caramelized Sweet Onion Dip

Makes 2 cups (450 g)

Skip the packet of onion dip mix with questionable ingredients because this quick DIY version will make your guests rave. It takes a few minutes to caramelize the onions but it makes a huge difference in the finished flavor. This classic dip can be served alongside veggies or works well in a bread bowl. To make this low-calorie, use reduced-fat sour cream and cream cheese in place of the full-fat versions.

GF　**NF**　**LS**

1 tablespoon (15 ml) olive oil
2 cups (320 g) sweet white or Vidalia
　onions, roughly chopped
1 clove of garlic, halved
¾ cup (173 g) sour cream
4 ounces (115 g) reduced-fat or regular
　cream cheese
½ teaspoon sea salt
⅛ teaspoon ground black pepper

1. Add the olive oil and onions to a skillet. Cook on medium-low heat until golden brown and translucent, about 15 minutes, taking care not to burn them. Let cool to room temperature.

2. Meanwhile, add the garlic, sour cream, cream cheese, sea salt, and black pepper to your blender container. Blend until smooth.

3. Add the cooled onions and pulse or blend on low for just a second to incorporate them into the mixture, leaving the chopped onions intact for texture. Be careful to not completely blend the onions into the dip. Pour into a bowl and let chill in the refrigerator for at least 1 hour for the flavors to meld and the dip to thicken. Serve.

Sun-Dried Tomato Spread

Makes 2 cups (450 g)

This spread is the ultimate crowd pleaser. Keep this recipe tucked away for your next party. You can use it as a spread, and it doubles as a dip, sandwich spread, or base for a pizza. If you end up loving the flavor, try adding ½ cup to 1 cup (120 to 235 ml) of water to the recipe for a tasty sauce to top your pasta dishes.

V **GF** **DF** **LS**

1 cup (140 g) raw unroasted cashews
¼ cup (60 ml) olive oil, plus more if needed
½ cup (55 g) sun-dried tomatoes packed in oil, chopped
2 tablespoons (28 ml) lemon juice
½ teaspoon sea salt
¼ teaspoon ground black pepper

1. Soak the cashews in a bowl of water for 2 hours and then drain and dump the water. This step is not absolutely necessary, but it makes a smoother, even textured spread.

2. Place the olive oil, sun-dried tomatoes, cashews, lemon juice, sea salt, and black pepper in your blender container.

3. Blend on low speed until combined and then blend on medium-high speed until completely smooth, using the tamper or stopping to scrape down the sides. Add more oil if necessary to reach your desired consistency. Serve.

☞ **SERVING TIP**

Serve this spread with crackers, vegetable chips, toast, as a base for a flatbread, or as a sandwich spread. It's great tossed in with scrambled eggs to add savory flavor.

Avocado Yogurt Dip

Makes 1½ cups (345 g)

Avocado is creamy, just like yogurt, so you can only imagine how luxurious and silky tasting this dip is. This whipped dip pairs well with cut-up veggies, crackers, or pita chips.

GF **NF** **LS**

1 cup (230 g) plain Greek yogurt
1 avocado, halved, pitted, peeled
1 clove of garlic, minced
2 tablespoons (28 ml) lemon juice
1 teaspoon sea salt
⅛ teaspoon ground black pepper

1. Add the Greek yogurt, avocado, garlic, lemon juice, sea salt, and black pepper to your blender container.

2. Blend on low to get the mixture moving and then on high until everything is fully combined and it has a whipped texture. Serve.

Mango Salsa

Makes 2 cups (320 g)

This salsa is ideal for an outdoor summer barbeque because it's bursting with crisp and fruity flavor. It's a great side dish or appetizer when paired with nachos, but I also find it works nicely as an accompaniment to steak, fish, or tacos. If you gently warm it on the stove, it transforms into a wonderful sauce that's perfect over chicken.

3 Roma tomatoes, quartered
1 large firm and ripe mango, pit removed, chopped (about 1 cup or 175 g chopped)
1 clove of garlic, minced
1 fresh jalapeño, seeds removed, chopped
¼ cup (4 g) fresh cilantro leaves, roughly chopped
2 tablespoons (28 ml) lime juice
¾ teaspoon sea salt

1. Place the tomatoes, mango, garlic, jalapeño, cilantro, lime juice, and sea salt in your blender container.

2. Pulse and then blend on low, until the tomatoes are chopped and the mixture is combined but still very chunky. Do not blend too much or it will be very watery. If you do overblend, hand chop another tomato and add it to the mixture or strain half of the mixture over a bowl with a fine-mesh strainer.

VARIATION: If you like very chunky salsa, add an additional ½ cup (90 g) of hand-chopped mango and tomatoes to the mixture after it is blended.

Smoky Vegan Veggie Dip

Makes 1 cup (246 g)

Cashews take the place of dairy in this dip that tastes smoky and slightly cheesy. It goes great with any veggie or cracker. The nutritional yeast adds important B vitamins to your diet.

¼ cup (60 ml) water
2 tablespoons (28 ml) fresh lemon juice
1 tablespoon (15 ml) gluten-free soy sauce, tamari, nama shoyu, or Bragg Liquid Aminos
½ cup (70 g) cashews
¼ cup (38 g) chopped red bell pepper
2 tablespoons (20 g) chopped red onion
2 tablespoons (8 g) nutritional yeast
1 clove of garlic, halved

1. Add the water, lemon juice, soy sauce, cashews, bell pepper, red onion, nutritional yeast, and garlic to your blender container.

2. Blend until completely smooth, adding more water, if necessary, to reach the desired consistency. Serve.

Simple Hummus ▶

Makes 1 cup (246 g)

If you're a hummus fan, this classic five-minute version will be something you whip up weekly. It is creamy, thick, and full of flavor. It makes a great sandwich spread, and it's a classic veggie dip. Bonus: It's chock-full of protein and healthy fats.

1 can (15 ounces, or 425 g) chickpeas, drained and rinsed (about 1⅓ cups, or 319 g)
1 clove of garlic
¼ cup (60 ml) olive oil
2 tablespoons (28 ml) water
2 tablespoons (28 ml) fresh lemon juice
2 tablespoons (30 g) tahini
½ teaspoon smoked paprika
½ teaspoon sea salt
Olive oil and paprika, for garnish

1. Add the chickpeas, garlic, olive oil, lemon juice, tahini, paprika, and sea salt to your blender container.

2. Blend until smooth and creamy, adding water if needed to reach the desired consistency.

3. Transfer to a bowl and garnish with a drizzle of olive oil and a shake of paprika. Serve.

Carrot Hummus

Makes 2 cups (about 500 g)

There's no better way to eat your veggies than in this beautifully orange-hued dip. Aim to impress with this gourmet-style, healthy hummus with a spicy kick. The carrots add a sweet flavor that is perfect for dipping pita chips or cucumber slices.

½ cup (120 ml) extra-virgin olive oil
2 tablespoons (28 ml) lemon juice
4 carrots, roasted (about 1 cup, or 130 g, chopped)
1 can (15 ounces, or 425 g) chickpeas, drained and rinsed (about 1⅓ cups, or 319 g)
1 tablespoon (15 g) tahini
½ teaspoon hot sauce
2 cloves of garlic, halved
½ teaspoon sea salt

1. Add the extra-virgin olive oil, lemon juice, roasted carrots, chickpeas, tahini, hot sauce, garlic, and sea salt to your blender container.

2. Blend until smooth and creamy, adding water if necessary to reach the desired consistency. Serve.

NOTE: To roast the carrots, preheat the oven to 375°F (190°C, or gas mark 5). Scrub and wash the carrots with water until clean. Place them in a baking dish, drizzle with olive oil, and roast for 1 hour or until soft. They should be tender and cooled before making the hummus.

Spicy Black Bean Dip

Makes 1 cup (250 g)

If you love black beans, try this version of bean dip! It packs a little heat from cayenne pepper and red pepper flakes. It has a milder bean flavor and a delightfully spicy finish. It's perfect for dipping and spreading.

1 can (15 ounces, or 425 g) black beans, drained and rinsed (about 1⅓ cups, or 319 g)
1 clove of garlic, halved
¼ cup (60 ml) olive oil
2 tablespoons (28 ml) fresh lemon juice
2 tablespoons (30 g) tahini
¼ teaspoon red pepper flakes
¼ teaspoon powdered cayenne pepper, or more to taste
½ teaspoon sea salt

1. Add the black beans, garlic, olive oil, lemon juice, tahini, red pepper flakes, cayenne pepper, and sea salt to your blender container.

2. Blend until smooth and creamy, adding water or more oil if needed to reach the desired consistency. Serve.

Tropical Guacamole

Makes 2 cups (about 450 g)

Whisk away to the tropics with this guacamole that includes a dash of sweet fruit. Pair it with a white fish and black beans for the ultimate meal with a little island flair.

V GF DF NF LS

2 small avocados, peeled and pitted
2 tablespoons (20 g) red onion, roughly chopped
1 clove of garlic, chopped
2 tablespoons (8 g) fresh parsley, chopped
2 tablespoons (2 g) fresh cilantro, chopped
½ teaspoon sea salt
⅛ teaspoon ground black pepper
2 tablespoons (28 ml) fresh lime juice
1 tablespoon (15 ml) olive oil
¼ cup (45 g) chopped mango
¼ cup (40 g) chopped pineapple, rind removed

1. Add the avocados, onion, garlic, parsley, cilantro, sea salt, black pepper, lime juice, and olive oil to your blender container.

2. Pulse and then slowly blend to gently combine until the mixture is mostly smooth, but still a little chunky.

3. Add the mango and pineapple. Pulse or blend on low for just a second to gently combine. Be careful to not blend the fruit into the mixture. It tastes best when left chopped throughout the mixture. Serve.

Kale Guacamole

Makes 1½ cups (about 340 g)

Kale is the king of greens, so why not try to sneak it into your guacamole? This one tastes heavenly and doesn't have a "green" flavor. It's beautifully creamy with gorgeous green specks of kale throughout. I like using lacinato kale for this recipe, but any variety will work. Try it in your black bean burrito.

V **GF** **DF** **NF** **LS**

2 small avocados, peeled and pitted
¼ cup (40 g) chopped white onion
1 clove of garlic, halved
⅓ cup (20 g) fresh parsley, chopped
1 teaspoon sea salt
1 tablespoon (15 ml) olive oil
2 tablespoons (28 ml) fresh lemon juice
⅛ teaspoon ground cayenne pepper, or
  more to taste
½ cup (34 g) kale, stems removed, chopped
3 tablespoons (45 g) sour cream (optional;
  omit for vegan or dairy-free options)

1. Add the avocados, onion, garlic, parsley, sea salt, olive oil, lemon juice, cayenne pepper, kale, and sour cream (if using) to your blender container.

2. Blend slowly until smooth and creamy, using the tamper to push the mixture into the blades or a spatula to scrape down the sides to redistribute the mixture. Serve.

Creamy Guacamole

Makes 1½ cups (about 340 g)

This classic guacamole is a daily staple in my home. I love how the blender ensures a perfectly whipped and smooth texture, even if your avocados are a little too firm. It's a wonderful addition alongside eggs or steak. Or serve it as the perfect little dip that it is—paired with tortilla chips and veggies. Use a full-bodied, fruity olive oil for the best flavor.

V **GF** **DF** **NF** **LS**

2 small avocados, peeled and pitted
¼ of a small onion, roughly chopped
1 clove of garlic, halved
⅓ cup (5 g) fresh cilantro
1 teaspoon sea salt
2 tablespoons (28 ml) fresh lime juice
1 tablespoon (15 ml) fruity extra-virgin
  olive oil
⅛ teaspoon powdered cayenne pepper
½ teaspoon ground black pepper

1. Add the avocados, onion, garlic, cilantro, sea salt, lime juice, olive oil, cayenne pepper, and black pepper to your blender container.

2. Blend slowly until smooth and creamy, using the tamper to push the mixture into the blades or a spatula to scrape down the sides to redistribute the mixture. Serve.

Spicy Cheese Guacamole

Makes 1½ cups (about 340 g)

I know you might be thinking that cheese + hot sauce in your guac is not something you'd normally do. Trust me on this one. You'll love the flavor and texture it brings to the table. Its presentation is beautiful as you catch the flecks of red pepper, yellow Cheddar, and green cilantro swimming in creamy avocado. It's the ultimate party-time dip and a perfect pairing to Taco Tuesday meals.

GF **NF** **LS**

2 small avocados, peeled and pitted
1 clove of garlic, minced
1 tablespoon (15 ml) hot sauce
½ teaspoon sea salt
1 tablespoon (15 ml) lime juice
½ teaspoon ground black pepper
¼ of a small onion, roughly chopped
½ cup (58 g) shredded Cheddar cheese
2 tablespoons (12 g) chopped scallions
1 red Fresno pepper, seeded and roughly chopped
⅓ cup (5 g) chopped fresh cilantro

1. Add the avocados, garlic, hot sauce, sea salt, lime juice, and black pepper to your blender container.

2. Blend slowly until smooth and creamy, but still a little chunky.

3. Add the onion, Cheddar cheese, scallions, Fresno pepper, and cilantro in that order. Pulse slowly or blend on low, using the tamper, until just combined, but not smooth. Serve.

Kalamata Olive Spread

Makes ¾ cup (225 g)

Kalamata olives are my favorite. They are salty and have so much full full-bodied flavor. This spread is amazing on sandwiches, as a veggie dip, or spread on toast.

GF **NF** **LS**

1 cup (100 g) pitted, unsalted Kalamata olives
3 cloves of garlic
1 tablespoon (15 ml) lemon juice
2 tablespoons (28 ml) olive oil
2 tablespoons (10 g) grated Parmesan cheese
2 tablespoons (8 g) fresh parsley, chopped

1. Add the Kalamata olives, garlic, lemon juice, olive oil, Parmesan cheese, and parsley to your blender container.

2. Pulse to combine and then blend until smooth. Serve.

Lemon Edamame Spread

Makes 1 cup (325 g)

One of my favorite things is edamame steamed in pods. The flavor is subtle, but it's amazing. If you enjoy that too, put this recipe on your list. This plush spread is satiny smooth and bursting with lemon flavor. It's ideal on sandwiches, sesame crackers, or as a thick veggie dip. It's beautifully bright green and makes a good choice to serve at a party. If you can't find fresh edamame, frozen and thawed works just fine.

¼ cup (60 ml) lemon juice
¼ cup (60 ml) olive oil
2 tablespoons (28 ml) water
1½ cups (255 g) shelled, cooked edamame
½ cup (32 g) fresh parsley
1 clove of garlic, chopped
1 tablespoon (16 g) miso paste
1 teaspoon sea salt
¼ teaspoon ground black pepper

1. Place the lemon juice, olive oil, water, edamame, parsley, garlic, miso, sea salt, and black pepper in your blender container.

2. Blend until smooth, using the tamper or stopping the machine and using a spatula to scrape down the sides and adding more water, 1 to 2 tablespoons (15 to 28 ml) at a time, if necessary, to reach the desired consistency. Serve.

Sun-Dried Tomato and Walnut Spread

Makes ¾ cup (225 g)

Walnuts make the perfect pesto spread when paired with sun-dried tomato—the nutty flavor complements it perfectly. This spread hits the spot on a roast beef sandwich, but can also double as an appetizer dip for bread or veggies. To transform this into a delicious pasta sauce, add an extra ¼ cup (60 ml) of olive oil to the recipe before blending.

GF **LS**

½ cup (50 g) walnuts
½ cup (55 g) sun-dried tomatoes, packed in oil
¼ cup (25 g) grated or shredded Parmesan cheese
2 cloves of garlic
¼ cup (60 ml) olive oil
¼ teaspoon sea salt

1. Place the walnuts, sun-dried tomatoes, Parmesan cheese, garlic, olive oil, and sea salt in your blender container.

2. Pulse the blender to first combine and then blend the ingredients on medium speed until the spread has a smooth but still chunky texture. Serve.

1. Add the roasted red peppers, cream cheese, garlic, parsley, and sea salt to your blender container.

2. Blend on medium-low speed until combined and fully whipped, stopping to scrape down the sides to redistribute the mixture. Serve.

Roasted Red Pepper Cream Cheese Spread ▶

Makes 1 cup (about 300 g)

You'll be in heaven with this homemade spread. This is so quick and easy to make that you'll be topping your bagels or toast with this luxurious cream cheese to amp up your morning. It's also perfect as a sandwich spread.

⅓ cup (60 g) roasted red peppers packed in water, drained
1 package (8 ounces, or 225 g) of cream cheese
1 clove of garlic, minced
1 tablespoon (4 g) fresh parsley, chopped
½ teaspoon sea salt

Garlic Artichoke Dip

Makes 1¼ cup (375 g)

This four-ingredient dip is a wonderful warm or chilled appetizer that tastes great on baguette slices. Its exceptionally creamy and smooth. Make it dairy-free by using vegan Parmesan cheese and vegan mayo in place of the regular versions.

½ cup (115 g) mayonnaise
1 can (14 ounces, or 390 g) artichokes packed in water, chopped and drained (about 1½ cups, or 450 g)
½ cup (50 g) grated Parmesan cheese
3 cloves of garlic, halved

1. Add the mayonnaise, artichokes, Parmesan cheese, and garlic to your blender container.

2. Blend until completely smooth, stopping to scrape down the sides to redistribute the mixture. Serve.

> ☞ **SERVING TIP**
>
> If you like warmed dips served, this is even better heated in the oven. Pour the mixture into an ovenproof dish. Bake at 375°F (190°C, or gas mark 5) for 15 to 20 minutes until warm and bubbly.

Basil Pesto Spread ▶

Makes 1 cup (about 260 g)

This rich, thick pesto spread is packed with flavor. You'll love spreading it on flax crackers and slices of cucumbers for a quick snack or appetizer.

¼ cup (60 ml) olive oil
1 cup (135 g) raw pine nuts
1 cup (40 g) fresh basil
2 cloves of garlic
1 teaspoon lemon juice
¼ cup (25 g) grated Parmesan cheese

1. Place the olive oil, pine nuts, basil, garlic, lemon juice, and Parmesan cheese in your blender container.

2. Blend on low until combined and then blend on medium-low until smooth but still gritty. Serve.

VARIATION: If you rather make a dairy-free spread that tastes cheesy without the dairy, omit the Parmesan cheese and add in 1 tablespoon (4 g) of nutritional yeast to the recipe.

Baba Ghanoush

Makes 1 cup (225 g)

Baba ghanoush has always been my dip of choice when frequenting Mediterranean restaurants. I love it's thick and chunky appeal, and it's fabulously vegan and gluten-free.

1 medium eggplant, peeled and cubed, about 3 cups (246 g)
2 tablespoons (28 ml) extra-virgin olive oil, for roasting
1 clove of garlic, halved
2 tablespoons (15 ml) lemon juice
3 tablespoons (45 g) tahini
½ teaspoon sea salt
2 tablespoons (8 g) chopped fresh parsley

1. Preheat the oven to high broil.

2. Sprinkle the eggplant with sea salt and place the cubed eggplant in a colander for 10 minutes to drain any excess liquid.

3. Pat dry with paper towels and spread evenly on an olive oil–greased baking sheet, tossing the eggplant in the oil. Roast for 5 to 10 minutes, turning once, until the eggplant is soft and browned.

4. Remove the eggplant from oven and let it cool for 5 minutes.

5. Add the eggplant, garlic, lemon juice, tahini, and sea salt to your blender container.

6. Blend until completely smooth and creamy.

Add in the parsley. Pulse or blend on low to gently combine. Serve.

Roasted Garlic White Bean Dip

Makes 1 cup (230 g)

This dairy-free dip can be made in mere minutes with your trusty blender. It's creamy and bursting with sweet garlic flavor, perfect for dipping baguette slices. Roasting the garlic gives it a sweet taste, which I find is popular with almost everyone. To speed up the time it takes to make this recipe, use store-bought roasted garlic. If you don't have cannellini beans, great northern beans can substitute.

2 tablespoons (28 ml) fruity olive oil
1 tablespoon (15 ml) lemon juice
1 can (15 ounces, or 425 g) cannellini beans, drained and rinsed (about 1½ cups, or 393 g)
5 roasted cloves of garlic
¼ teaspoon sea salt
⅛ teaspoon ground black pepper

1. Place the olive oil, lemon juice, cannellini beans, roasted garlic, sea salt, and black pepper to your blender container.

2. Blend until smooth, using the tamper or stopping and using a spatula to scrape down the sides and redistribute the mixture. Serve.

NOTE: To roast the garlic, preheat the oven to 400°F (200°C, or gas mark 6). Peel and discard the papery outer layers of the garlic bulb. Cut ¼ to ½ inch (6 to 12 mm) from the top of the bulb. Place the garlic cut-side up in a baking dish. Drizzle with olive oil. Cover with aluminum foil and roast for 35 minutes until golden and the cloves feel soft when pressed. Let cool before using the cloves in the white bean dip.

Raw "Ricotta" Cheese

Makes 1 cup (200 g)

If dairy-free is your vibe, this is a must-have recipe. This raw ricotta is heavenly on warm baguettes out of the oven, topped with homemade jelly. Use it to make Italian dishes or in a breakfast bowl topped with fresh, chopped fruit and berries.

V GF DF LS

1 cup (135 g) raw unroasted macadamia nuts
3 tablespoons (45 ml) lemon juice
¼ cup (60 ml) water
½ teaspoon sea salt

1. Add the macadamia nuts, lemon juice, water, and sea salt to your blender container.

2. Blend until mostly smooth, with a little texture. Add more water, 2 tablespoons (28 ml) at a time, to reach the desired consistency, if needed. Serve.

Creamy Crab Dip

Makes 2 cups (425 g)

This seafood dip can be served chilled or warm. It's very creamy and rich, a perfect indulgent addition to any party appetizer list. I find it pairs well with whole wheat crackers or celery sticks.

 GF NF LS

¼ cup (60 g) sour cream
8 ounces (225 g) cream cheese
¼ teaspoon crab boil spice, such as Old Bay seasoning
½ teaspoon hot sauce
1 clove of garlic, halved
1 tablespoon (15 ml) lemon juice
½ teaspoon sea salt
⅛ teaspoon ground black pepper
8 ounces (225 g) crabmeat
2 tablespoons (8 g) fresh parsley

1. Place the sour cream, cream cheese, crab boil spice, hot sauce, garlic, lemon juice, sea salt, and black pepper in your blender container. Blend until fully combined and smooth.

2. Add the crabmeat and parsley to the blender. Blend on low until combined, using the tamper to move the mixture along or a spatula to scrape the sides and redistribute the mixture. If you like a very smooth dip, blend until the crab is completely mixed and creamy within the dip. If you like a chunky dip, only blend on low a few seconds until gently combined. Serve.

◄ Chicken Spread

Makes 2½ cups (530 g)

Spreads like this are great to make at the beginning of each week to grab for a fast meal when you're short on time. Use this protein spread to top crackers, make chicken sandwiches perfect for a picnic, or add a scoop to leafy green salads. Whenever I'm traveling, I pack a wrap stuffed with this spread and it keeps extremely well until I'm ready to enjoy it. It's savory, smoky flavor is so satisfying. It's also perfect for those on a low-carb, low-sugar diet.

GF **NF** **LS**

8 ounces (225 g) cream cheese
¼ cup (60 g) mayonnaise
½ teaspoon onion powder
½ teaspoon garlic powder
½ teaspoon sea salt
⅛ teaspoon cayenne pepper
¼ teaspoon smoked paprika
2 cups (280 g) cooked chopped chicken
   breast, about 2 medium chicken breasts
½ cup (50 g) chopped celery

1. Add the cream cheese, mayonnaise, onion powder, garlic powder, sea salt, cayenne pepper, and smoked paprika to your blender container. Blend until smooth and combined.

2. Add the chicken breast and celery. Blend on low, using a tamper to push the mixture into the blades or a spatula to scrape down the sides until combined. Serve.

☞ **SERVING TIP**

If you like warmed dips served with a baguette, this is fantastic when heated in the oven. Pour the dip mixture into an ovenproof dish. Bake at 350°F (180°C, or gas mark 4) for 10 minutes until warm.

Spinach and Artichoke Dip

Makes 2 cups (450 g)

This dip is heavy on the veggies and amazing served out of a bread bowl. It's usually a favorite at get-togethers. The dip is great chilled or slightly warmed, the way it will be right after making it.

1 tablespoon (15 ml) olive oil
⅓ cup (53 g) chopped shallot
1 package (10 ounces, or 280 g) of frozen, thawed, and drained spinach
1 cup (300 g) jarred or canned artichoke hearts, chopped and drained
½ cup (115 g) mayonnaise
½ cup (115 g) sour cream
¼ cup (25 g) grated Parmesan cheese
½ teaspoon sea salt
¼ teaspoon ground black pepper

1. Over a medium skillet, add the olive oil. Sauté the shallots, spinach, and artichoke hearts until cooked and heated through. Let cool slightly.

2. Meanwhile, add the mayonnaise, sour cream, Parmesan cheese, sea salt, and black pepper to your blender container. Blend until smooth and combined.

3. Add the spinach-artichoke mixture to the blender and pulse gently or blend on low for just a few seconds until gently combined, taking care not to overblend because this dip is best chunky. Serve.

Mushroom and Bacon Dip

Makes 1½ cups (250 g)

While this dip is on the heavier side, it's great to entertain guests with on special occasions. The flavors are complex and exciting, and it's a hit every time. Its chunky texture works well served with bagel or pita chips.

4 slices of sugar-free bacon
2 cups (140 g) chopped white button mushrooms
¼ cup (40 g) chopped shallot
4 ounces (115 g) Neufchatel or low-fat cream cheese
½ cup (115 g) sour cream
2 cloves of garlic, halved
½ teaspoon sea salt
½ teaspoon ground black pepper

1. Cook the bacon until crispy, reserving 1 tablespoon (15 ml) of fat. Pat the bacon dry and roughly chop it.

2. Add the reserved bacon fat to a medium skillet and add the mushrooms and shallots. Sauté until caramelized and soft, about 15 minutes. Let cool slightly.

3. Meanwhile, add the Neufchatel cheese, sour cream, garlic, sea salt, and black pepper to your blender container. Blend until smooth.

4. Add the mushroom-shallot mixture and chopped bacon to your blender container. Pulse or blend on low a few seconds until gently combined but not smooth. Pour in a bowl and let chill in the refrigerator for at least 1 hour. Serve.

Salmon Mousse

Makes 6 servings

Before my wedding reception, we had an amazing appetizer table full of scrumptious foods for our guests to enjoy while the wedding party took photos. One of everyone's favorites was hollowed out cucumber cups stuffed with salmon mousse. I remember thinking that I was so happy with the caterer for dreaming up this fun finger food. I loved it so much I created my own mousse, and it remains a perfect appetizer and snack to this day. It's also great served with crackers or baguette slices.

GF **NF** **LS**

3 tablespoons (45 ml) cold water
1 teaspoon unflavored gelatin
1 cup (230 g) sour cream
4 ounces (115 g) smoked salmon, roughly
  chopped
1 tablespoon (15 ml) lemon juice
¼ teaspoon sea salt

1. In a small saucepan, combine the cold water and gelatin, stirring to combine. Let the gelatin soften for 5 minutes. Gently heat over medium-low heat until dissolved. Let cool for a minute.

2. Meanwhile, place the sour cream, salmon, lemon juice, and sea salt to your blender container. Blend until combined.

3. While the blender motor is running on a low speed, pour the gelatin mixture in through the lid spout and blend until combined. Then, blast on high to make sure it is extremely smooth.

4. Pour the mixture into a bowl, without mixing. Cover with plastic wrap and let chill in the refrigerator for at least 2 hours. Serve.

7

ALL-PURPOSE SAUCES, PESTOS, AND CONDIMENTS

What do you do when you need to make a spectacular meal, but are short on time? Make a fabulous topping, sauce, or dip that instantly elevates your dish. There's no better way to use your blender than for everyday sauces and condiments. I find they're a game changer to enhance your daily meals. From making homemade sauces for your pastas, dipping sauces for appetizers, condiments for your sandwiches, or a sweet sauce for desserts, you'll love whipping up seemingly gourmet versions for yourself.

Tahini Sauce

Makes ¾ cup (175 ml)

This Mediterranean-inspired sauce makes almost anything taste amazing. Use it on falafel, burgers, sandwiches, wraps, and salads. You can also serve it as a dip in a bowl with a drizzle of extra-virgin olive oil plus a shake of cayenne pepper to create a beautiful presentation. The heat from the cayenne also adds to the flavor.

½ cup (120 ml) water
2 tablespoons (28 ml) lemon juice
½ cup (120 g) tahini
½ teaspoon sea salt
½ teaspoon chopped garlic

1. Place the water, lemon juice, tahini, sea salt, and garlic in your blender container.

2. Blend on medium-high speed until completely combined and smooth, adding more water if necessary. Serve or store in an airtight container in the refrigerator.

Garlic Aioli

Makes 1 cup (about 235 g)

Every time I travel to Spain I get one of my favorite dishes: *patatas aioli*. It is fried potatoes with delicious garlic aioli sauce drizzled on top, and it's out of this world. Since I don't travel there too often, I created my own homemade version. You can use garlic aioli for many dishes as a dipping sauce or a replacement for regular mayo. It's rich, flavorful, and garlicky. Use a high-quality olive oil for this recipe.

2 teaspoons (28 ml) lemon juice
1 whole egg
4 cloves of garlic, minced
1 cup (235 ml) olive oil
¼ teaspoon sea salt
⅛ teaspoon ground black pepper

1. Add the lemon juice, egg, and garlic your blender container. Blend until fully combined.

2. While the machine is running on a medium-low speed, slowly stream in the olive oil. Be sure to stream it in very slowly, as this is the key to making a good mayonnaise. Blend until it is a smooth emulsion.

3. Add the sea salt and black pepper and blend on low for a few seconds to gently combine. Serve or store in an airtight container in the refrigerator.

Olive Oil Mayo

Makes 1 cup (225 g)

There's nothing like homemade mayo! This recipe is a classic, and it is luxuriously silky smooth. Making mayonnaise with your blender is an experiment with the science of emulsion. It might take more than one attempt to master this, but once you do, there's no going back to store-bought. While this recipe imparts a light olive flavor, it works well in any recipe you'd like to add mayo to. If you prefer the flavor of avocado oil or grapeseed oil better, this recipe also works well with those substitutions.

1 egg yolk
1 teaspoon Dijon mustard
1 teaspoon lemon juice
½ tsp sea salt
⅛ teaspoon ground white pepper
1 cup (235 ml) olive oil

1. Add the egg yolk, Dijon mustard, and lemon juice to your blender container.

2. Blend until smooth. While the machine is still running on a low speed, add in the olive oil very slowly. Process until a smooth, thick consistency is reached. It is very important to drizzle the oil in slowly or it will not emulsify. The slower you pour the oil, the thicker the mayo will be. If you pour fast, the mayo will be runny. If this happens, it can usually be saved by adding one more egg yolk to the mixture.

3. Add in the sea salt and white pepper to taste. Blend again. Serve or store in an airtight container in the refrigerator.

Honey Mustard Dipping Sauce

Makes ¾ cup (170 g)

This amazing dipping sauce floats on both the sweet and savory side. It is a staple condiment in my house. It's fabulous for chicken tenders, fries of any kind, and pretzels. I've even used this as a salad dressing.

¼ cup (85 g) honey
¼ cup (60 g) mayonnaise
¼ cup (60 g) Dijon mustard
1 tablespoon (28 ml) white wine vinegar

1. Add the honey, mayonnaise, Dijon mustard, and white wine vinegar to your blender container.

2. Blend until smooth. Serve or store in an airtight container in the refrigerator.

Hot Mustard ▶

Makes 1 cup (225 g)

Once you make your own spicy mustard, you probably won't be going back to store-bought. Mustard enhances many recipes from dipping pretzels or simply amping up a sandwich. Experiment by adding extra spices to this recipe to make different flavors of mustard.

⅓ cup (59 g) mustard seeds
½ cup (120 ml) water
¼ cup (60 ml) white wine vinegar
1 tablespoon (20 g) maple syrup
1 teaspoon ground turmeric
½ teaspoon sea salt
⅛ teaspoon cayenne pepper

1. Add the mustard seeds to bowl and pour the water on top to cover them. Let them sit for 2 hours.

2. Once the mustard seeds are done soaking, add the bowl of mustard seeds with the water, white wine vinegar, maple syrup, turmeric, sea salt, and cayenne pepper to your blender container.

3. Blend slowly until smooth and it reaches a paste consistency, adding more water if necessary. Serve or store in an airtight container in the refrigerator.

1. Add the water, tomato paste, white wine vinegar, maple syrup, onion powder, garlic powder, and sea salt.

2. Blend until a completely smooth paste forms. The ketchup is great out of the blender, but for a richer flavor and thicker paste, simmer the ketchup on the stove for 15 minutes until warm and cooked. Let cool. Serve or store in an airtight container in the refrigerator.

Vegan Aquafaba Mayo

Makes ¾ cup (about 170 g)

You'll be pleasantly surprised with this vegan mayo that is super easy to make. It tastes just like the real thing minus the preservatives you'll get in the store-bought vegan mayo. If you prefer to use olive oil instead of grapeseed oil, that works well in this recipe, too.

1 teaspoon apple cider vinegar
½ teaspoon ground mustard
½ teaspoon sea salt
1 teaspoon maple syrup
3 tablespoons (45 ml) liquid from a can of
  chickpeas plus 5 cooked chickpeas
¾ cup (175 ml) grapeseed oil

▲ Classic Ketchup

Makes 1 cup (about 240 g)

Everyone needs a quick ketchup recipe. This one is easy and much lower in sugar than you'd see in the store-bought brands.

V GF DF NF

¼ cup (60 ml) water
1 can (6 ounces, or 170 g) plain tomato paste
¼ cup (60 ml) white wine vinegar
¼ cup (80 g) maple syrup
¼ teaspoon onion powder
⅛ teaspoon garlic powder
1 teaspoon sea salt

1. Add the apple cider vinegar, mustard, sea salt, maple syrup, chickpea liquid, and chickpeas to your blender container. Blend until combined.

2. While the machine is running on medium-low speed, slowly stream in the grapeseed oil, stopping once the mixture is thick. Be sure to stream it in very slowly, as this is the key to making a good mayonnaise. Serve or store in an airtight container in the refrigerator.

1. Add the tomato ketchup, maple syrup, white wine vinegar, Worcestershire sauce, hot sauce, paprika, and cayenne pepper to your blender container.

2. Blend until smooth and fully combined. Serve or store in an airtight container in the refrigerator.

Maple Barbecue Sauce

Makes 1 cup (about 250 g)

Some barbecue sauces take a long time to make, but I prefer this quick version made with tomato ketchup. Many store-bought barbecue sauces have corn syrup and a crazy amount of sugar, and I love that I can control that in this sauce. Try it slathered on any meat you're going to grill, as a dipping sauce, or mixed in to pulled pork for tacos.

V **GF** **DF** **NF**

¾ cup (180 g) plain tomato ketchup
2 tablespoons (40 g) maple syrup
1 tablespoon (15 ml) white wine vinegar
1 tablespoon (15 ml Worcestershire sauce
¼ teaspoon hot sauce
2 teaspoons paprika
⅛ teaspoon cayenne pepper

Tomato Sauce

Makes 2 cups (about 245 g)

If you've ever checked the nutrition label, you'll have noticed that store-bought tomato sauce is very high in sugar. This tomato sauce is my mom's classic recipe. It's so easy and tastes phenomenal, sans all the sugar and preservatives. There's no need to remove the skins or seeds from the tomatoes; they add a nice texture once cooked through. For the red wine, I find that cabernet sauvignon tastes the best.

V   GF   DF   NF

1 small shallot, finely chopped
1 tablespoon (15 ml) olive oil
3 tablespoons (48 g) tomato paste
6 medium Roma tomatoes, chopped
2 cloves of garlic, chopped
⅛ teaspoon sugar
3 tablespoons (45 ml) red wine
2 teaspoons capers
1 teaspoon dried basil
1 teaspoon dried parsley
¼ teaspoon sea salt
⅛ teaspoon ground black pepper

1. Add the shallots and olive oil to a stockpot. Cook until the shallots are translucent, about 5 minutes. Mix in the tomato paste.

2. Meanwhile, place the tomatoes, garlic, and sugar in the blender container. Blend until smooth and fully combined.

3. Transfer the blender mixture to the stockpot. Add in the red wine, capers, basil, parsley, sea salt, and black pepper.

4. Simmer on low, uncovered, for about 15 minutes until it has thickened nicely. For a richer flavor, add 2 tablespoons (10 g) of Parmesan cheese. Serve or store in an airtight container in the refrigerator.

Vegan Pink Sauce

Makes 3½ cups (about 850 g)

This recipe is exceptionally easy, but you'll need a stockpot to cook a portion of it. I prefer this creamy sauce that is just like vodka sauce, without the vodka, over traditional tomato sauce in my pasta dishes. It's amazing over any type of rice pasta.

2 tablespoons (28 ml) extra-virgin olive oil
3 cloves of garlic, minced
1 can (28 ounces or 785 g) crushed tomatoes
¼ teaspoon ground black pepper
½ cup (70 g) raw unroasted cashews
1 teaspoon sea salt
½ cup (120 ml) water

1. Place a stockpot on the stove. Add the olive oil and garlic. Cook for 1 minute. Add the crushed tomatoes and black pepper. Let simmer.

2. Meanwhile, place the cashews, sea salt, and water in your blender container.

3. Blend until the mixture is completely smooth. If you find that you're having trouble blending the cashews smooth, add ½ cup (about 120 ml) of the tomato mixture from the stockpot to the blender and blend together until the cashews are fully combined.

4. Add the cashew cream to your stockpot and mix to combine. Let simmer until heated through, about 5 to 10 minutes. This will be a slightly chunky sauce, but if you'd like a very smooth sauce, transfer the pink sauce to your blender in batches and blend until very smooth.

5. Serve or store in an airtight container in the refrigerator.

☞ **BLENDING TIP**

Warm sauces or soups expand when blended. When blending anything hot, be sure to only fill your container up half way to give the sauce room to expand. To make this easy, blend in batches and transfer each batch back to a large bowl once blended.

Cauliflower Alfredo Sauce

Makes 1½ cups (185 g)

If you love alfredo, this is a must-try sauce. It's made with low-calorie cauliflower—not milk—and is silky smooth. People love it! This sauce tastes best warmed, and you'll adore it served over pastas like fettuccine, steamed broccoli, or zucchini noodles. While fresh cauliflower is best in this recipe, using frozen cauliflower that's been fully defrosted also works well.

GF **LS**

4 cups (400 g) chopped cauliflower florets, about one head of cauliflower
2 tablespoons (28 ml) olive oil
2 tablespoons (28 g) butter
4 cloves of garlic, minced
½ teaspoon ground white pepper
½ teaspoon sea salt
¼ cup (60 ml) almond milk
¼ cup (25 g) grated Parmesan cheese

1. In a large pot of boiling water, cook the cauliflower florets until soft, about 10 minutes.

2. When the cauliflower is soft, drain the liquid and place the cauliflower in your blender container.

3. Add the olive oil, butter, garlic, white pepper, sea salt, almond milk, and Parmesan cheese to the blender.

4. Blend on high until smooth and creamy, adding more almond milk to make it the consistency you'd like. Because the cauliflower was cooked, the sauce will be warm and ready to serve out of the blender. Serve or store in an airtight container in the refrigerator.

> ☞ **SERVING TIP**
>
> Mix Cauliflower Alfredo Sauce into cooked rice. Add chopped and cooked vegetables to make an easy weeknight casserole dish. The alfredo sauce can also be used as a pizza sauce.

Mushroom Cream Sauce

Makes 2 cups (245 g)

Mushrooms work so well in sauces, and they are high in folic acid and vitamin D. This thick sauce takes minutes to make and works great over pasta, zoodles, or in a green bean casserole. My favorite way to serve this sauce is over a bowl of fettuccine noodles sprinkled with Parmesan cheese. Because it's so rich and flavorful, a little goes a long way, and you won't have to use much in your dish.

½ cup (80 g) chopped shallots
2 tablespoons (28 ml) olive oil
16 ounces (455 g) white mushrooms, stems
  removed, chopped
1 teaspoon sea salt
¼ teaspoon ground black pepper
1 cup (235 ml) heavy whipping cream, plus
  more if needed

1. Heat a sauté pan over medium-high heat.
Place the shallots and olive oil in the pan
and cook until soft and translucent, about
5 minutes.

2. Add the mushrooms, sea salt, and black
pepper to the pan and cook until the juices
evaporate and the mushrooms are cooked
through, about 10 minutes. Let it cool
a minute.

3. Add the mushroom-shallot mixture and
heavy cream to your blender container. Blend
until smooth and creamy, adding more cream
if needed to reach your desired consistency.
Add more sea salt or black pepper to taste.
The mixture will be warm, but if you'd like
it hotter, return it to your pan and heat the
sauce on low until warm, but do not boil.

4. Serve or store in an airtight container in
the refrigerator.

VARIATION: To make this dairy-free and
vegan, simply replace the heavy whipping
cream with unsweetened full-fat canned
coconut milk.

Arugula Lemon Pesto

Makes 1½ cups (about 390 g)

Why not get arugula into your sauce and
healthify your meal a bit? If you like the light
bitterness of arugula, you'll really like this
recipe. In fact, you might even find people
who don't like arugula adore it, too.

1 cup (235 ml) olive oil
3 tablespoons (45 ml) lemon juice
3 cloves of garlic, halved
½ cup (68 g) raw pine nuts
4 cups (80 g) fresh arugula, loosely packed
1 cup (40 g) fresh basil, loosely packed
½ cup (50 g) grated Parmesan cheese
½ teaspoon sea salt
½ teaspoon ground black pepper

1. Add the olive oil, lemon juice, garlic, pine
nuts, arugula, basil, Parmesan cheese, sea salt,
and black pepper to your blender container.

2. Blend until smooth and combined. If you'd
like a smoother sauce, add more olive oil until
you reach your desired consistency.

3. Serve or store in an airtight container in
the refrigerator.

Creamy Cashew Cheese Sauce

Makes 2 cups (250 g)

I love cashew-based cheese sauces. I make this often to go on top of pasta or steamed broccoli. It's rich and has a silky texture that's to die for. You can serve this warmed as a pasta sauce or chilled over a cold pasta or potato salad. If you're a vegan making a pasta dish for a non-veggie friend, serve them this sauce. It's always a winner.

(V) (GF) (DF) (LS)

1 cup (140 g) raw cashews
1 cup (235 ml) almond milk, plus more
  if needed
¼ cup (15 g) nutritional yeast
1 teaspoon garlic powder
1 teaspoon onion powder
⅛ teaspoon mustard powder
½ teaspoon sea salt
¼ teaspoon ground black pepper
¼ teaspoon cayenne pepper

1. Place the cashews, almond milk, nutritional yeast, garlic powder, onion powder, mustard powder, sea salt, black pepper, and cayenne pepper in your blender container.

2. Blend on high until completely smooth, adding more almond milk if necessary to create the desired consistency. Use less milk for a thicker sauce and more milk for a thinner sauce. Serve or store in an airtight container in the refrigerator.

☞ BLENDING TIP

Power blenders allow you to blend dry ingredients like nuts without soaking them first. Although if you have time, soaking the nuts helps to create a silky-smooth consistency for sauces. If you are using a regular blender for this recipe or other recipes using dry nuts, soak the nuts in water for a minimum of 2 hours. Discard the water before using the nuts.

☞ SERVING TIP

Try this sauce drizzled on top of a warm baked potato with fresh chives.

Basil Pesto Sauce

Makes 1¼ cup (325 g)

The first time I had basil pesto was at my mother-in-law's house, and with every glorious bite, I wondered how I had never had this delicious sauce before that moment. Since then, I've been in love with it and look forward to her dinners made with it. I've now adapted my own version that is quick, easy, and reminds me of hers.

GF **LS**

1 cup (235 ml) extra-virgin olive oil, plus more if needed
2 cups (80 g) fresh basil, loosely packed
3 cloves of garlic
¼ cup (35 g) pine nuts
1 cup (100 g) grated Parmesan cheese
¼ teaspoon sea salt
¼ teaspoon ground black pepper

1. Add the olive oil, basil, garlic, pine nuts, Parmesan cheese, sea salt, and black pepper to your blender container.

2. Pulse to gently combine and then blend on high until completely smooth and creamy, adding in more olive oil if necessary to reach the desired consistency. This is good thick or runny, so make it according to your needs.

3. Serve or store in an airtight container in the refrigerator.

Basil Walnut Pesto

Makes 1½ cups (about 390 g)

Perfect as a pasta sauce or as an alternative tomato sauce, I make this often and use it as a sandwich spread. Or try it drizzled on ravioli or steamed veggies. It's a family favorite.

GF **LS**

1 cup (235 ml) olive oil
5 cloves of garlic, halved
½ cup (50 g) raw walnuts
2 cups (80 g) fresh basil leaves, loosely packed
½ cup (50 g) grated Parmesan cheese
1 teaspoon sea salt
½ teaspoon ground black pepper

1. Add the olive oil, garlic, walnuts, basil, Parmesan cheese, sea salt, and black pepper to your blender container.

2. Blend until smooth and combined. If you'd like a thinner pesto, add more olive oil until you reach your desired consistency. Serve or store in an airtight container in the refrigerator.

> ☞ **SERVING TIP**
>
> If using pesto on pasta or zucchini noodles, prepare the pasta and use 1 tablespoon (15 g) of pesto per serving.

½ cup (130 g) creamy peanut butter
1 cup (235 ml) unsweetened full-fat canned coconut milk
2 tablespoons (28 ml) fresh lime juice
1 tablespoon (15 ml) gluten-free soy sauce, tamari, nama shoyu, or Bragg Liquid Aminos
2 pitted medjool dates
1 teaspoon minced ginger
2 cloves of garlic, chopped
½ teaspoon red pepper flakes

1. Add the peanut butter, coconut milk, lime juice, soy sauce, dates, ginger, garlic, and red pepper flakes to your blender container.

2. Blend on high until extremely smooth, scraping down the sides as necessary.

3. Serve or store in an airtight container in the refrigerator.

Green Pea Pesto

Makes 2½ cups (640 g)

If you want to make a quick, healthy pesto but don't have basil, reach for the stash of green peas in your freezer. This pesto tastes fresh and is good on anything you decide to slather it on. It's a sauce that's on the sweeter side, and it also doubles as a great party dip after chilling. I love it mixed with rigatoni or on a vegetable sandwich made with roasted vegetables, sprouts, and melted cheese.

▲ Peanut Coconut Sauce

Makes 1½ cups (190 g)

This sauce . . . it's simply amazing. Who wouldn't love the combo of peanut + coconut together? I enjoy a drizzle of this Asian-inspired sauce over rice noodles or as a dipping sauce for egg rolls or pot stickers.

1 cup (235 ml) olive oil, plus more if needed
3 cloves of garlic
½ cup (68 g) raw pine nuts
3 cups (450 g) fresh green peas or (390 g)
  frozen and thawed
½ cup (50 g) grated Parmesan cheese
½ teaspoon ground black pepper
½ teaspoon sea salt

1. Add the olive oil, garlic, pine nuts, peas, Parmesan cheese, black pepper, and sea salt to your blender container.

2. Blend until completely smooth. If you'd like a thinner sauce, add more olive oil until you reach your desired consistency.

3. Serve or store in an airtight container in the refrigerator.

Jalapeño Pepper Sauce

Makes 1 cup (130 g)

My husband loves spicy sauces, but I'm not a huge fan. I've learned to love this one because it's not too spicy and it also has a nice sweetness to balance out the heat. This DIY version is perfect for dipping, spreading, or drizzling on whatever you think needs a little bit more flavor. Try it drizzled on scrambled eggs or fish tacos.

2 tablespoons (28 ml) olive oil
½ cup (120 ml) white wine vinegar
1 cup (150 g) chopped green bell pepper,
  about 1 pepper
½ cup (80 g) chopped onion
3 cloves of garlic, halved
2 green jalapeños, roughly chopped, most
  of the seeds removed
¼ cup (15 g) fresh parsley
¼ teaspoon sea salt

1. Place the olive oil, white wine vinegar, bell pepper, onion, garlic, jalapeños, parsley, and sea salt in your blender container.

2. Blend until smooth. Serve or store in an airtight container in the refrigerator.

☞ **SERVING TIP**

Make this into a spicy mayo you can use on sandwiches and as a dipping sauce by whisking together 2 tablespoons (16 g) of this hot pepper sauce into ¼ cup (60 g) of mayo.

Green Enchilada Sauce

Makes 2½ cups (310 g)

If you're not a big fan of tomato-based sauces, this Mexican-inspired sauce might be your choice on top of Latin dishes. This mild-flavored green sauce is my favorite on chicken enchiladas or white Cheddar enchiladas. I guarantee this is a keeper, and you'll find a lot of ways to use it, including dipping nachos into it as a green salsa dip. If you like spicy sauces, keep the seeds on the jalapeño.

V **GF** **DF** **NF** **LS**

1 can (28 ounces, or 785 g) tomatillos, drained, about 3 cups (396 g)
1 jalapeño pepper, seeds removed, chopped
2 cloves of garlic, chopped
½ cup (80 g) onion, chopped
½ cup (8 g) fresh cilantro
1 teaspoon sea salt
¼ teaspoon ground black pepper

1. Add the tomatillos, jalapeño, garlic, onion, cilantro, sea salt, and black pepper to your blender container.

2. Pulse to combine and then blend until smooth. If you like your enchilada sauce with a chunkier texture, watch it carefully as it blends smooth rather quickly.

3. If you'd like this warmed, simmer in a saucepan on medium-low heat until warm. Serve or store in an airtight container in the refrigerator.

Red Enchilada Sauce

Makes 3½ cups (430 g)

I never really ate enchiladas until I moved to Texas. Now, they are a weeknight staple, so I had to develop my own sauce. I use this red sauce primarily on enchiladas, but it also works well drizzled on shredded chicken or loaded nachos and tacos, too.

1 can (28 ounces, or 785 g) diced tomatoes, about 3 cups (720 g)
1½ tablespoons (11 g) chile powder
1½ tablespoons (11 g) taco seasoning
½ cup (80 g) chopped onions
2 cloves of garlic, halved
1 jalapeño, ribs and seeds removed
½ teaspoon sea salt

1. Place the tomatoes, chile powder, taco seasoning, onions, garlic, jalapeño, and sea salt together in your blender container.

2. Blend until smooth. Serve or store in an airtight container in the refrigerator.

☞ **SERVING TIP**

For a delicious meal, toss this sauce with shredded chicken breast to serve on tacos.

Buffalo Yogurt Dipping Sauce

Makes 1 cup (120 g)

This five-minute yogurt sauce is fantastic over a cold, chopped veggie salad or as a dipping sauce for homemade oven fries or chicken tenders.

1 cup (230 g) plain Greek yogurt
1 tablespoon (15 ml) apple cider vinegar
2 tablespoons (28 ml) hot sauce
1 tablespoon (15 ml) safflower oil
½ teaspoon sea salt
½ teaspoon onion powder
¼ teaspoon garlic powder
1 teaspoon dried parsley
½ teaspoon dried dill
¼ teaspoon ground black pepper

1. Add the Greek yogurt, apple cider vinegar, hot sauce, safflower oil, sea salt, onion powder, garlic powder, parsley, dill, and black pepper to your blender container.

2. Blend until smooth. Pour in a bowl and chill in the refrigerator for 30 minutes to thicken.

3. Serve or store in an airtight container in the refrigerator.

Dark Chocolate Sauce

Makes 1¼ cups (about 300 g)

Sweet and gooey chocolate sauce is a dream topping and tastes utterly decadent. This version is sweetened with dates and has a bittersweet flavor that is fantastic on anything from banana sundaes to fruit. It's good served chilled or gently warmed.

1 cup (235 ml) almond milk
⅔ cups (53 g) unsweetened cocoa powder
2 teaspoons vanilla extract
6 pitted medjool dates

1. Add the almond milk, cocoa powder, vanilla, and dates to your blender.

2. Pulse to break up the dates and then blend on high until smooth and warm, about 2 to 3 minutes.

3. Serve or store in an airtight container in the refrigerator.

Alfredo Sauce

Makes 2 cups (250 g)

Rich and creamy, this easy to whip up alfredo is perfect for coating angel hair pasta or for making chicken stand out. It's also great in a scalloped potato casserole or lasagna. Personally, my favorite way to eat this is over spaghetti squash noodles for a low-carb dinner.

1 cup (235 ml) 1% organic milk
8 ounces (225 g) cream cheese
1 tablespoon (8 g) arrowroot flour
½ teaspoon sea salt
3 cloves of garlic, minced
1 tablespoon (14 g) butter
½ cup (50 g) grated Parmesan cheese,

1. Add the milk, cream cheese, arrowroot flour, sea salt, garlic, and butter to your blender container. Blend until smooth.

2. Transfer the mixture to a saucepan and heat over medium-high heat for a few minutes. Add the Parmesan cheese to the saucepan, stirring constantly, until warm and thickened, about 5 minutes.

3. Serve or store in an airtight container in the refrigerator.

☞ **TIP**

Arrowroot flour is a healthy alternative to cornstarch for thickening to sauces.

Pineapple Teriyaki Sauce

Makes ¾ cup (90 g)

This easy teriyaki sauce is made with pineapple and honey instead of the traditional cane sugar, which makes it feel so island-esque. It tastes great on chicken, fish, or beef. You can also use it as a dipping sauce or for scrumptious stir-fry dishes.

GF **DF** **NF**

¼ cup (60 ml) gluten-free soy sauce, tamari, nama shoyu, or Bragg Liquid Aminos
¼ cup (60 ml) water
1 tablespoon (8 g) arrowroot powder
4 tablespoons (85 g) honey
3 tablespoons (45 ml) rice wine vinegar
4 tablespoons (60 g) crushed or (40 g) diced pineapple
2 tablespoons (28 ml) pineapple juice
1 clove of garlic, chopped
1 teaspoon fresh minced ginger

1. Place the soy sauce, water, arrowroot powder, honey, rice wine vinegar, pineapple, pineapple juice, garlic, and ginger in your blender container.

2. Blend until completely combined and smooth.

3. Transfer the mixture to a small saucepan and bring the sauce to a boil. Reduce the heat to medium and simmer, whisking frequently, until thickened, about 5 minutes.

4. Serve or store in an airtight container in the refrigerator.

Salted Date Caramel Sauce

Makes 1 cup (240 g)

I know you love caramel sauce because who doesn't? This version uses dates instead of corn syrup or white sugar, and it is perfect drizzled on top of apple slices or your homemade ice cream and desserts. It'll soon be your secretly healthier way to satisfy a sweet tooth. The juicer your dates are, the better.

 **V** **GF** **DF** **NF**

20 pitted medjool dates
1½ cups (355 ml) water, plus more if needed
1 teaspoon vanilla extract
¼ teaspoon sea salt

1. Place the dates, water, vanilla, and sea salt in your blender container.

2. Pulse the blender to break up the dates and then blend on high until smooth, using the tamper or stopping to scrape down the sides. Add more water to get to desired consistency. Depending on how fresh and gooey your dates are, you might have to add quite a bit more water.

3. Serve or store in an airtight container in the refrigerator.

Vegan Sour Cream

Makes 1 cup (about 240 g)

This vegan sour cream is perfect for tacos, Mexican dishes, on top of a baked potato, or for thickening up pasta sauces with a cream. I promise you'll love this so much you'll make it every week so you have a batch on hand for pretty much anything you eat. While you don't have to soak the cashews, it makes for a more silky and creamy sour cream. If you don't have time to soak them, you'll just need to add more water to the recipe.

1 cup (140 g) raw cashews
½ cup (120 ml) water, plus more if needed
¼ cup (60 ml) lemon juice
½ teaspoon apple cider vinegar
½ teaspoon sea salt
1 teaspoon nutritional yeast

1. Place the cashews in a bowl and fill it with water, covering them completely. Soak for 2 to 6 hours. Discard the water, reserving the cashews.

2. Add the water, lemon juice, apple cider vinegar, cashews, sea salt, and nutritional yeast to your blender container.

3. Blend on high until completely smooth and creamy. Serve or store in an airtight container in the refrigerator.

Chimichurri Sauce

Makes 1 cup (175 g)

Chimichurri is a popular, herby, pesto-like condiment that comes to us from Argentina. It's a fantastic sauce accompaniment to any meat, particularly beef, chicken, or fish, because it's light and full of fresh flavor. It's always an ideal choice for serving at your next barbecue.

½ cup (120 ml) safflower or walnut oil (omit for nut-free option)
¼ cup (60 ml) red wine vinegar
1 teaspoon sea salt
1 teaspoon ground black pepper
¼ teaspoon cayenne pepper
2 teaspoons chile powder
1 teaspoon oregano
3 cloves of garlic, chopped
½ cup (30 g) fresh parsley, loosely packed
½ cup (8 g) fresh cilantro, loosely packed

1. Place the safflower oil, red wine vinegar, sea salt, black pepper, cayenne pepper, chile powder, oregano, garlic, parsley, and cilantro in your blender container.

2. Blend on low or quickly pulse to chop the herbs and gently combine the ingredients.

3. Serve or store in an airtight container in the refrigerator.

8

DRESSINGS, VINAIGRETTES, MARINADES, AND SPICE BLENDS

They say that the dressing really makes the salad and that's the truth. From a traditional green salad to a scrumptious pasta salad, you're going to love making your own. Most of us eat salads because they're a healthful and delicious meal. Typical store-bought dressings are loaded with sugar, preservatives, and chemicals, which isn't healthful or tasty at all. Fresh, homemade dressings taste much better, can be made to your own taste, and can often do double-duty as marinades or dipping sauces. Never ruin a salad again with a bad dressing.

◂ Watermelon Vinaigrette

Makes 1 cup (235 ml)

Sunny, beachy, and light describes this vinaigrette perfectly! I'm a huge watermelon fan, so this one is at the top of my list. Despite watermelon's sweetness, this dressing isn't supersweet. Pair it on a salad with a generous helping of crumbled feta, cucumbers, and chopped mint. Or try it with my favorite, a green salad topped with grilled Halloumi cheese.

1 cup (150 g) seedless chopped watermelon, rind removed
1 tablespoon (10 g) minced shallot
⅛ teaspoon cayenne pepper
1 tablespoon (15 ml) lime juice
1 tablespoon (20 g) honey
2 tablespoons (28 ml) olive oil
½ teaspoon sea salt
¼ teaspoon ground black pepper

1. Place the watermelon, shallot, cayenne pepper, lime juice, honey, olive oil, sea salt, and black pepper in your blender container.

2. Blend until combined and smooth.

3. Serve or store in a sealed glass or ceramic jar in the refrigerator.

Sesame Soy Vinaigrette

Makes 1 cup (235 ml)

Sweet and delightfully spicy, you're going to love this on your next Asian-inspired green salad topped with sprouts and grated carrots or my personal favorite, tossed in a cold noodle bowl topped with oven-roasted, sliced shiitake mushrooms and fresh chives.

V **GF** **DF** **NF**

2 tablespoons (28 ml) sesame oil
2 tablespoons (28 ml) gluten-free soy sauce, tamari, nama shoyu, or Bragg Liquid Aminos
¼ cup (36 g) coconut sugar
½ cup (120 ml) lime juice
½ cup (120 ml) safflower oil
½ teaspoon sea salt
⅛ teaspoon ground black pepper
¼ teaspoon chile flakes

1. Place the sesame oil, soy sauce, lime juice, coconut sugar, safflower oil, sea salt, and black pepper in your blender container.

2. Blend until combined and emulsified. Next, add in the chile flakes and gently mix with a spoon to combine.

3. Serve or store in a sealed glass or ceramic jar in the refrigerator.

☞ **BLENDING TIP**

The blender is perfect for dressings that include oils + vinegars or juice because they help to emulsify the mixture better than what you could with a whisk, ensuring a dressing that doesn't separate later. To emulsify in your blender, blend on low and increase to the highest speed. Let the machine run for at least 20 seconds until the dressing is completely combined.

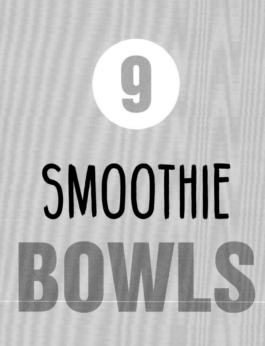

9

SMOOTHIE
BOWLS

If you're looking for a new way to eat light and healthy, try a colorful smoothie bowl for your next meal. These bowls are always a burst of brightness for your palate because they include both a smoothie portion plus an impressive list of mouthwatering toppings like fruit, healthful spices, nuts, and seeds. It's a perfect way to incorporate extra superfoods and vitamin-rich fruit into your diet.

Loaded Baked Potato Soup

Makes 8 servings, about 8 cups (1.9 L)

This potato soup is lusciously thick and smooth. When topped with any variety of chopped bacon and chives, it tastes just like a decadent loaded baked potato. It's a winner with any crowd and makes a fabulous stand-alone meal. No one will know it's dairy-free! This makes a large batch, perfect for a family meal or stashing leftovers in the freezer for a rainy day.

V **GF** **DF** **NF** **LS**

4 russet potatoes
1 chopped white onion
2 chopped celery stalks
2 teaspoons olive oil, divided
½ cup (120 ml) unsweetened rice or almond milk (omit for dairy-free option)
4 cups (946 ml) chicken broth (omit for vegan option) or Vegetable Broth (page 193)
1 teaspoon Himalayan sea salt
½ teaspoon ground black pepper
1 clove of garlic, halved
Bacon, chives, and sour cream, for topping (optional)

1. Preheat the oven to 400°F (200°C, or gas mark 6).

2. Rinse the potatoes and prick them with a fork. Place them on a pan and drizzle about a teaspoon of olive oil on the potatoes. Sprinkle them with sea salt. Bake them in the oven for 1 hour or until soft and cooked through.

3. Meanwhile, add the onion, celery, and 1 teaspoon of olive oil to a stockpot. Cook until softened, about 5 minutes.

4. When the potatoes are done, remove the peel and mash them lightly it in a bowl.

5. Add the milk, broth, sea salt, black pepper, and garlic to the stockpot. Add the mashed potatoes. Bring to a boil, turn off the stove, and let it cool for a few minutes.

6. Transfer the mixture to a large blender container in batches. Blend on low for 30 seconds and then bring the speed up to high and blend for 60 seconds until smooth and fully combined. Do this for each batch, placing the blended batches back into the stockpot.

7. Pour into bowls and sprinkle with toppings, if desired. Serve.

☞ BLENDING TIP

When blending hot batches of soup in your blender, never fill the container more than halfway full. Hot soups expand once blended and need room at the top of your container to allow for expansion.

Broccoli Cheddar Soup ▶

Makes 2 servings, about 2 cups (475 ml)

Broccoli and cheese soup was one of the first soups I made with my power blender, and if you've never made soup with yours, this is a great option to start with. I always have these ingredients on hand, so this is a go-to recipe for me. Feel free to use frozen broccoli if that is all you have—just make sure you thaw it first.

GF **NF** **LS**

4 cups (320 g) broccoli florets, fresh or
   thawed from frozen
1 cup (235 ml) Vegetable Broth (page 193)
   or chicken broth (plus more, optional)
¼ teaspoon sea salt
¼ teaspoon ground black pepper
⅛ teaspoon garlic powder
3½ ounces (100 g) chopped sharp Cheddar
   cheese, about 1 cup

1. Add the broccoli, broth, sea salt, black pepper, garlic, and Cheddar cheese to your blender container. Add more broth if you like a thinner soup.

2. Pulse the blender to gently get the mixture moving. Then, blend until completely combined and very smooth, about 1 to 3 minutes.

3. To heat the soup, add it to a stockpot and warm the soup on medium-low heat for about 10 minutes. If you have a Vitamix or Blendtec, you can heat the soup right in the blender container; blend on high for 6 to 8 minutes until steaming hot. Serve.

Cucumber Yogurt Soup

Makes 3 servings, about 3 cups (700 ml)

This delicious chilled soup is perfect for when the hot weather strikes and you want a cool meal. This is also a good one to have when eating lighter before and after a cleanse. It's extremely satisfying but also light.

2 cucumbers, chopped, equal to 2 cups (270 g)
2 cups (230 g) plain Greek yogurt, 0% milkfat
1 Hass avocado, pit and peel removed
1 clove of garlic, halved
1½ teaspoons sea salt
¼ teaspoon ground black pepper
¼ teaspoon onion powder
2 tablespoons (8 g) fresh parsley
1 tablespoon (15 ml) lemon juice

1. Add the cucumbers, Greek yogurt, avocado, garlic, sea salt, black pepper, onion powder, parsley, and lemon juice to your blender container.

2. Blend until smooth, about 1 minute. Because of the avocado, this does not keep well for longer than a few hours, so you'll want to enjoy it shortly after making.

Pumpkin Soup

Makes 3 servings, about 3 cups (700 ml)

When the fall hits, I love to consume foods that have pumpkin. I make this soup every year around Thanksgiving and it's always a hit. It's a sweet, salty, and thick soup that is especially satisfying in the winter months.

1½ cups (355 ml) low-sodium chicken broth (omit for vegan option) or Vegetable Broth (page 193)
½ cup (120 ml) unsweetened full-fat canned coconut milk
1½ cups (368 g) canned pumpkin
½ cup (80 g) sweet white onions, sautéed until soft and translucent
2 cloves of garlic, halved
2 fresh pitted medjool dates
¼ teaspoon cinnamon
½ teaspoon ground nutmeg
1 teaspoon sea salt
¼ teaspoon ground black pepper

1. Add the broth, coconut milk, pumpkin, sautéed onions, garlic, dates, cinnamon, nutmeg, sea salt, and black pepper to your blender container.

2. Blend until smooth, about 1 to 3 minutes.

3. To heat the soup, add it to a stockpot and warm the soup on medium-low heat for about 10 minutes. If you have a Vitamix or Blendtec, you can heat the soup right in the blender container; blend on high for 6 to 8 minutes until steaming hot. Serve.

Sun-Dried Tomato and Roasted Red Pepper Soup ▶

Makes 2 servings, about 2 cups (475 ml)

Do you love soup-and-salad or soup-and-sandwich combination meals? If so, then this is your go-to. This soup is one of my favorites to pair alongside a vinaigrette topped salad or a small sandwich. It is easily made from jarred ingredients, and it's full-bodied flavor is addictive.

V **GF** **DF** **NF**

⅓ cup (37 g) jarred sun-dried tomatoes, packed in oil
2 cloves of garlic, halved
½ cup (90 g) jarred roasted red bell peppers, packed in water
1 quartered Roma tomato
½ cup (80 g) chopped and sautéed sweet white onion
1 cup (235 ml) chicken broth (omit for vegan option) or Vegetable Broth (page 193)
¼ teaspoon ground black pepper
1 teaspoon sea salt
1 fresh pitted medjool date

1. Add the sun-dried tomatoes, garlic, roasted bell peppers, Roma tomato, sweet onion, broth, black pepper, sea salt, and date to your blender container.

2. Blend until the mixture is smooth and creamy, about 1 to 3 minutes.

3. To heat the soup, add it to a stockpot and warm the soup on medium-low heat for about 10 minutes. If you have a Vitamix or Blendtec, you can heat the soup right in the blender container; blend on high for 6 to 8 minutes until steaming hot. Serve.

☞ **TIP**

It's easy to save blended soups in the freezer for consuming at a later date. To maximize space, simply place the soup in a quart (946 ml) or gallon (3.8 L) size plastic freezer bag and seal tightly. Label it and store it flat on a shelf.

Black Bean Soup

Makes 4 servings, about 4 cups (946 ml)

Black bean soup is a classic that pairs well with sandwiches or is a star all on its on. Top with sour cream and scallions for extra flavor and a beautiful presentation.

(V) (GF) (DF) (NF) (LS)

1½ cups (355 ml) low-sodium Vegetable Broth (page 193) or chicken broth (omit for vegan option)
2 cans (15 ounces, or 425 g, each) black beans, 3 cups, (720 g) cooked, rinsed, drained
½ cup (80 g) chopped and sautéed Vidalia or sweet white onions
2 cloves of garlic
2 tablespoons (28 ml) fresh lime juice
¼ teaspoon ground cumin
¼ teaspoon cayenne pepper
½ teaspoons sea salt
¼ teaspoons ground black pepper

1. Add the broth, black beans, sautéed onions, garlic, lime juice, cumin, cayenne pepper, sea salt, and black pepper to your blender container.

2. Blend until smooth, about 1 to 3 minutes.

3. To heat the soup, add it to stockpot and warm the soup on medium-low heat for about 10 minutes. If you have a Vitamix or Blendtec, you can heat the soup right in the blender container; blend on high for 6 to 8 minutes until steaming hot. Serve.

☞ BLENDING TIP

If you like chunky soups, add in extra vegetables or beans after you've blended the soup and pulse them with the soup to roughly chop and incorporate them into the recipe. It creates a nice texture and a thicker soup.

Cream of Asparagus Soup

Makes 3 servings, about 3 cups (700 ml)

While asparagus isn't my favorite vegetable, I simply adore it in this soup. This quick and easy recipe is one of my staple favorites when asparagus is in season, and it's a perfect stand-alone meal paired with some toasted bread.

(GF) (NF) (LS)

2 cups (268 g) fresh chopped asparagus, woody stems removed
1½ cups (355 ml) water
2 cups (475 ml) low-sodium chicken broth or Vegetable Broth (page 193)
¼ teaspoon sea salt
¼ teaspoon cayenne pepper
¼ teaspoon garlic powder
2 tablespoons (28 g) unsalted butter
¼ cup (60 ml) heavy cream

1. In a stockpot over medium heat, cook the asparagus in the water for about 10 minutes or until soft.

2. Add the asparagus with the water, broth, sea salt, cayenne pepper, garlic powder, butter, and heavy cream to your blender container.

3. Blend until very smooth, about 1 to 3 minutes.

4. It should be fairly warm from the cooked asparagus, but to heat the soup further, add it to a stockpot and warm the soup for about 10 minutes. If you have a Vitamix or Blendtec, you can heat the soup right in the blender container; blend on high for 6 to 8 minutes until steaming hot. Serve.

Shiitake Mushroom Bisque

Makes 3 servings, about 3 cups (700 ml)

Shiitake mushrooms are magical. They are meaty and abundantly flavorful, and when they are roasted or panfried, they can make any dish taste fantastic. Once you transform these beauties into a creamy soup, you'll come back to it again and again.

V **GF** **DF** **NF** **LS**

2 tablespoons (28 g) butter or (28 ml) olive oil
¼ cup (40 g) white onion, chopped
2 cups (140 g) chopped white mushrooms, stems removed
2 cups (140 g) chopped shiitake mushrooms, stems removed

2 cups (475 ml) Vegetable Broth (page 193) or chicken broth (omit for vegan option)
2 cloves of garlic, halved
½ teaspoons sea salt
¼ teaspoon ground black pepper
1 tablespoon (15 ml) gluten-free soy sauce, tamari, nama shoyu, or Bragg Liquid Aminos
1 tablespoon (15 ml) heavy cream (optional; omit for dairy-free option)

1. In a stockpot over medium heat, sauté the onions, white mushrooms, and shiitake mushrooms in butter or olive oil until soft, about 15 to 20 minutes.

2. Transfer the shiitake mixture to your blender container. Add the broth, garlic, sea salt, black pepper, soy sauce, and heavy cream (if using).

3. Blend until smooth, about 1 to 2 minutes. It will be hot from the mushroom mixture, but to heat the soup further, add it to a stockpot and warm the soup for about 10 minutes. If you have a Vitamix or Blendtec, you can heat the soup right in the blender container; blend on high for 6 to 8 minutes until steaming hot. Serve.

☞ BLENDING TIP

Soup recipes that call for heavy cream can be substituted with an equal amount of coconut cream taken from the top of a can of full-fat coconut milk. The consistency and richness is extremely similar.

Creamy Corn Chowder

Makes 4 servings, about 4 cups (946 ml)

Thick and sweet, this corn chowder is a classic, and it's wonderful in the winter months. Add chopped, cubed chicken breast as a topping to garnish your bowls to make this a complete and filling meal.

V **GF** **NF** **LS**

2 tablespoons (28 g) butter
½ cup (80 g) chopped sweet white onion
1 russet potato, cooked, skin removed
2 cups (475 ml) low-sodium chicken broth
   (omit for vegan option) or Vegetable Broth
   (page 193)
2 cups (about 328 g) sweet yellow or white
   corn, thawed from frozen or fresh cut
   from ears of corn (divided)
⅛ teaspoon cayenne pepper
1 teaspoons sea salt
¼ teaspoon paprika

1. Add the butter and onions to a sauté pan and sauté for about 5 minutes until translucent. Remove from the heat and let it cool for 1 minute.

2. Add the broth, onions, 1½ cups (246 g) of the corn, potato, cayenne, sea salt, and paprika to your blender container.

3. Blend until smooth, about 1 to 2 minutes. Add in the remaining ½ cup (82 g) of corn and pulse once or blend on low for 2 seconds until combined but not smooth.

4. It should be fairly warm from the onion-and-butter mixture, but to heat the soup further, add it to a stockpot and warm the soup for about 10 minutes. If you have a Vitamix or Blendtec, you can heat the soup right in the blender container before adding in the remaining ½ cup (82 g) of corn; blend on high for 6 to 8 minutes until steaming hot. Serve.

Ajo Blanco Soup ▷

Makes 3 servings, about 3 cups (700 ml)

My husband and I travel to the Andalusian region of Spain, and one of my favorite meals is their garlic and almond chilled soup. It's a fantastically easy blender recipe full of healthy fat that will keep you full all day. This rich soup is best served in small portions. Be sure to use a good quality olive oil. To save time, you can use store-bought blanched almonds.

1 cup (145 g) blanched almonds
1 cup (235 ml) Spanish olive oil
2 cloves of garlic, chopped
1 teaspoon sherry vinegar
1 teaspoon sea salt
1½ cups (355 ml) water, plus more if needed
Apple slices and red grapes (optional)

1. Place the almonds, olive oil, garlic, sherry vinegar, and sea salt in your blender container.

2. Blend until smooth. With the motor still running on medium speed, add in the water through the lid until the water is fully combined with the rest of the soup mixture. If you don't have a lid spout and can't do this, add in the water and blend until very smooth, about 1 to 3 minutes.

3. Pour into a bowl and chill in the refrigerator until ready to serve. It is a very thick soup, but if it appears too thick, add more water. Garnish with apple slices and red grapes, if desired.

NOTE: To blanch the almonds, place them in a heatproof bowl. Pour boiling water over top and let sit for 5 minutes. Then, use your hands to squeeze the almonds out of the skins.

Coconut Cauliflower Soup

Makes 4 servings, about 4 cups (946 ml)

This creamy soup is one-part savory, one-part coconutty. It's a unique twist on cauliflower soups, and I have a feeling you'll love it if you are a fan of this cruciferous vegetable. Serve with a garnish of brown butter, sautéed chopped cauliflower florets, or freshly chopped chives.

GF **NF** **LS**

3 tablespoons (42 g) unsalted butter
¼ cup (40 g) white onions, chopped
1 large head of cauliflower florets, about
  4 cups (400 g) chopped
2½ cups (570 ml) low-sodium chicken broth,
  divided
1 cup (235 ml) full-fat canned coconut milk
1½ teaspoons sea salt

1. In a large stockpot, add the butter and onions. Cook over medium-low heat. Sauté, stirring occasionally until the onions become translucent, about 5 minutes.

2. Add the cauliflower and 2 cups (475 ml) of the broth to the stockpot. Bring to a low boil, then reduce to a simmer and allow to cook for about 15 to 20 minutes until the cauliflower is tender.

3. Remove from the heat, let cool for 1 minute, and transfer the mixture into your blender container.

4. Add in the coconut milk, sea salt, and remaining ½ cup (120 ml) of broth.

5. Blend until the soup is smooth and creamy, about 1 to 2 minutes. The soup will be fairly warm due to the cooked cauliflower mixture. To heat the soup further, add it to a stockpot and warm the soup for about 10 minutes. If you have a Vitamix or Blendtec, you can heat the soup right in the blender container; blend on high for 6 to 8 minutes until steaming hot. Serve.

Spinach and Broccoli Soup

Makes 3 servings, about 3 cups (700 ml)

If eating greens like broccoli and spinach is difficult for you, you might like consuming them in this meal. This green-hued soup tastes cheesy, has very little dairy, and is very low calorie. Serve it garnished with garlic toasted croutons.

GF **NF** **LS**

2 tablespoons (28 ml) olive oil
2 tablespoons (20 g) white onion, chopped
2 cups (160 g) fresh or thawed from frozen
  broccoli, chopped
2 cups (60 g) fresh spinach
2 cloves of garlic, minced
1½ cups (355 ml) low-sodium chicken broth
  or Vegetable Broth (page 193)

¼ cup (30 g) shredded Parmesan cheese
¼ teaspoon ground black pepper
½ teaspoon sea salt
3 tablespoons (45 g) plain 0% Greek yogurt

1. Heat the olive oil in a stockpot. Add the onions, broccoli, spinach, and garlic. Cook for 5 to 10 minutes until cooked through and soft.

2. Add the vegetable mixture, broth, Parmesan cheese, black pepper, sea salt, and Greek yogurt to your blender container.

3. Blend until smooth, about 1 to 2 minutes. The soup will be fairly warm due to the cooked vegetable mixture. To heat the soup further, add it to a stockpot and warm the soup for about 10 minutes. If you have a Vitamix or Blendtec, you can heat the soup right in the blender container; blend on high for 6 to 8 minutes until steaming hot. Serve.

Tomato, White Bean, and Basil Soup

Makes 3 servings, about 3 cups (700 ml)

If you love tomato soup and basil, this soup is heaven. The white beans make it thick and creamy without added calories or dairy. Serve garnished with croutons and shredded mozzarella cheese.

(V) (GF) (DF) (NF) (LS)

3 tablespoons (45 ml) olive oil
2 tablespoons (20 g) chopped white onion
3 cloves of garlic, minced
1 tablespoon (16 g) tomato paste
2 tomatoes, quartered, seeds removed
1 can (15 ounces, or 425g) white cannellini beans, rinsed and drained, about 1½ cups (393 g)
1 cup (235 ml) low-sodium Vegetable Broth (page 193) or chicken broth (omit for vegan option)
1 teaspoon sea salt
1 teaspoon dried basil
¼ teaspoon crushed red pepper flakes

1. Heat the olive oil in a stockpot. Add the onion and garlic. Cook until the onion is softened and translucent, about 5 minutes. Let it cool for 1 minute.

2. Add the tomato paste, tomatoes, cannellini beans, broth, sea salt, basil, red pepper flakes, and onion-garlic-oil mixture to your blender container.

3. Blend until smooth, about 1 to 2 minutes. To heat the soup, add it to a stockpot and warm the soup on medium-low heat for about 10 minutes. If you have a Vitamix or Blendtec, you can heat the soup right in the blender container; blend on high for 6 to 8 minutes until steaming hot. Serve.

Coconut Strawberry Dessert Soup

Makes 3 servings, about 3 cups (700 ml)

This delightful soup can be a palate cleansing dessert or a light meal. This tastes just like strawberry coconut shortcake, so if you have a sweet tooth, you'll love this blend. It's lovely garnished with finely chopped mint, orange zest, or Coconut Whipped Cream (page 250).

GF **NF**

2 cups (340 g) strawberries, sliced
½ cup (115 g) 0% plain Greek yogurt
½ cup (120 ml) orange juice
1 tablespoon (20 g) honey
½ cup (120 ml) full-fat canned coconut milk
½ teaspoon vanilla extract
¼ teaspoon fresh minced ginger
¼ teaspoon ground cinnamon

1. Place the strawberries, Greek yogurt, orange juice, honey, coconut milk, vanilla, ginger, and cinnamon in your blender container.

2. Blend until fully combined and smooth, about 1 minute.

Garlicky White Bean Soup

Makes 3 servings, about 3 cups (700 ml)

There's nothing better on a cold winter day than a warm bowl of white bean soup. This garlic-infused version is nothing short of pure flavor, and it goes great with a sliced and lightly toasted baguette. I use fresh garlic, but if you have roasted garlic on hand, that's even better in this recipe.

GF **NF** **LS**

2 tablespoons (28 g) butter
1 tablespoon (15 ml) olive oil
¼ cup (40 g) chopped shallots
2 cloves of garlic, chopped, plus more to taste
1 can (15 ounces, or 425 g) cannellini beans, drained and rinsed (about 1½ cups, or 393 g)
1 cup (235 ml) low-sodium chicken broth or Vegetable Broth (page 193)
1 teaspoon sea salt
¼ teaspoon ground black pepper

1. Add the butter, olive oil, shallots, and garlic to a stockpot. Cook until the shallots are soft and translucent, about 5 minutes.

2. Meanwhile, add the beans, broth, sea salt, and black pepper to your blender container. When the onions are done, add the mixture to the blender.

3. Blend the mixture until smooth, about 1 minute. The soup is thick, but if you want it thinner, add more broth to the mixture. Add more garlic to taste.

4. To heat the soup, add it back to the stockpot and warm the soup for about 10 minutes. If you have a Vitamix or Blendtec, you can heat the soup right in the blender container; blend on high for 6 to 8 minutes until steaming hot. Serve.

☞ BLENDING TIP

Typically, blended soups are naturally thick and rich compared to their broth heavy counterparts. After making a soup recipe in your blender, add more water or broth to make the texture to your liking.

Gazpacho Andaluz

Makes 3 servings, about 3 cups (700 ml)

Whenever I travel to Spain, I have this soup almost every day—it's that good. I made my own version so that when I'm not traveling, I can still enjoy it. It's super easy and because it's chilled, there is no cooking involved. It's a thick, heavy soup, and it can easily serve as a full meal. If you don't have sherry vinegar, substitute a good quality balsamic or red wine vinegar. Use only fresh tomatoes, not canned, and a fruity olive oil. Garnish with chopped hard-boiled eggs, chopped cucumber, and a drizzle of extra-virgin olive oil, right over the top.

V **GF** **DF** **NF** **LS**

5 tomatoes, chopped, seeds removed, about 2 ½ cups (450 g) chopped
2 ounces (55 g) white bread, fresh or day-old (use gluten-free bread for gluten-free option)
2 cloves of garlic
½ cup (120 ml) fruity olive oil
2 tablespoons (28 ml) sherry vinegar
1 teaspoon sea salt
Hard-boiled eggs (omit for vegan option) and chopped cucumber, for garnish

1. Add the tomatoes, bread, garlic, olive oil, sherry vinegar, and sea salt to your blender container.

2. Blend until smooth and completely combined, about 1 to 2 minutes. It is an extremely rich and thick soup. If you'd like it lighter, add some water and blend again. It's best to chill it overnight in the refrigerator to allow the flavors to develop.

3. When ready to serve, pour into a bowl. Garnish with hard-boiled eggs (if using) and cucumber.

☞ BLENDING TIP

Tomato seeds often cause recipes to form a froth when blended. Remove the seeds before blending tomatoes to achieve a recipe with a smoother texture.

Socca

Makes one 9-inch (23 cm) round socca

Socca is a naturally gluten-free chickpea flour pancake that can be served with a variety of toppings. Top with avocado slices and chopped arugula or top it with a fried egg. This basic recipe can be made quickly in your blender and is completely versatile.

1¼ cup (285 ml) water
3 tablespoons (45 ml) olive oil
1 cup (120 g) chickpea flour
½ teaspoon sea salt
½ teaspoon ground black pepper
1 teaspoon olive oil, to coat pan

1. Add the water, olive oil, chickpea flour, sea salt, and black pepper to your blender container. Blend until smooth and creamy.

2. Transfer the mixture to a large bowl. Cover the bowl and let it sit for 12 to 24 hours.

3. Place a heavy 9-inch (23 cm) cast iron skillet in the oven. Preheat the oven to 425°F (220°C, or gas mark 7).

4. Remove the skillet from oven and add 1 teaspoon of olive oil to the pan to coat or spray lightly with oil. Pour the socca batter onto the skillet. Bake for 10 minutes until firm and the edges are set.

5. Turn on the broiler for 2 minutes to set the top. Remove from the oven and cut into wedges. Serve hot out of the pan as is or with toppings of choice.

Falafel Patties

Makes 3 large burgers or 6 small patties

Chickpeas, also called garbanzo beans, make hearty burgers or sliders, just serve them on a bun with tzatziki sauce. They are also good as a protein side to a salad. This batter can also double as falafel balls to use as a veggie meatball or in a pita.

1 can (15 ounces, or 425 g) chickpeas, drained and rinsed (about 1½ cups [360 g])
2 tablespoons (30 g) tahini
½ cup (30 g) fresh parsley, roughly chopped
2 whole eggs
1 cup (96 g) gluten-free old-fashioned oats
4 cloves of garlic, peeled and cut in half
1 teaspoon sea salt
½ teaspoon pepper
¼ teaspoon ground cumin
¼ teaspoon paprika
Olive oil, for frying

1. Add the chickpeas, tahini, parsley, eggs, oats, garlic, sea salt, black pepper, cumin, and paprika to your blender container.

2. Blend slowly on medium-low until fully combined, using the tamper to press the mixture into the blades or a spatula to scrape down the sides and redistribute the mixture.

3. Form the mixture into 3 large or 6 small even patties, depending on the size you'd like, placing them on a plate when formed.

4. Heat olive oil in a large skillet over medium heat. Fry the patties until golden and crisp, about 3 minutes on each side.

Panfried Mushroom Ravioli

Makes about 50 ravioli

Ravioli can be time consuming, but not when you use wonton wrappers. These taste rich and delicious. Served as a meal or as an appetizer, these are sure to be a hit with anyone who loves mushrooms.

NF **LS**

2 tablespoons (28 ml) olive oil
16 ounces (455 g) white mushrooms
½ cup (80 g) chopped shallots
½ teaspoon sea salt
¼ teaspoon ground black pepper
¼ cup (15 g) fresh flat-leaf parsley
½ cup (125 g) ricotta cheese
¼ cup (25 g) Parmesan cheese, plus extra
  for serving
1 package of wonton wrappers
Olive oil, for frying and serving

1. Heat a large skillet over medium-high heat. Add the olive oil, mushrooms, and shallots. Cook until the mushrooms are brown and the shallots are translucent and cooked through.

2. Add the sea salt, black pepper, and parsley. Cook for 1 minute more. Let cool for a minute.

3. Transfer the mushroom-shallot mixture to your blender container. Blend until combined.

4. Add the ricotta and Parmesan cheese. Pulse or blend on low until just combined.

5. Lay out the wonton wrappers on a large work surface. Add 1 teaspoon of the ravioli mixture onto one side of each wonton wrapper. Using a brush, apply water along the edges of the wrapper. Fold over and seal with your finger, pressing the sides shut and working out any air bubbles. Continue until all of the ravioli filling is gone, placing them on a plate when done.

6. Heat a skillet with olive oil. Fry the ravioli in batches of 6 to 8 for 2 minutes on each side or until cooked through. Serve the ravioli hot with tomato sauce or a drizzle of extra-virgin olive oil and Parmesan cheese.

VARIATION: If you rather not panfry your raviolis, then you can boil them in water. Bring a large pot of water to boil. Reduce to a simmer and place 8 ravioli at a time into the pot. Cook for 4 to 5 minutes, remove with a slotted spoon, and drain before serving.

Whole Wheat Margherita Pizza

Makes one 12-inch (30 cm) pizza crust

Who doesn't love pizza? I know I do and it's one of my favorite meals. This recipe uses your blender to make the batter smooth and easy. This basic recipe is your Friday night go-to idea.

FOR THE CRUST

1½ cups (355 ml) milk, dairy or almond (omit for nut-free option)
1 whole egg
½ cup (120 ml) safflower oil
1 teaspoon sea salt
1 cup (120 g) whole wheat flour
1 cup (125 g) white whole wheat flour
½ tablespoon (7 g) baking powder

FOR THE PIZZA

¼ cup (61 g) pizza sauce or (65 g) tomato paste
3 ounces (85 g) fresh sliced mozzarella cheese
6 to 8 basil leaves (optional)
Grated Parmesan cheese (optional)
Sea salt, ground black pepper, and Italian spice blend to taste

1. Preheat the oven 400°F (200°C, or gas mark 6).

2. Add the milk, egg, oil, sea salt, and baking powder to your blender container. Blend until combined. While the blender is running on medium-low speed, pour the flour through the lid opening. Blend on low to medium speed to fully combine.

3. Pour the batter onto a 12-inch (30 cm) round pizza pan lined with parchment paper. Using a spatula, spread the batter evenly in a round circle. Bake for 15 minutes.

4. Remove the crust from the oven. Using a soft spatula, spread the pizza sauce on the pizza crust. Add the mozzarella slices on top of the sauce and then the basil leaves and Parmesan cheese (if using). Season to taste.

5. Put the pizza back in the oven and bake for 5 minutes or until cheese is melted.

VARIATIONS

White flour dough: If you don't like whole wheat flour, substitute the 2 cups (250 g) of flour with the same amount of unbleached all-purpose flour in it's place.

Gluten-free dough: Replace the 2 cups (250 g) of flour with the same amount of a gluten-free 1 to 1 baking flour.

Mashed Chickpea Lettuce Wrap

Makes 6 servings

Whether you're a vegetarian or not, there's no disputing that this wrap tastes amazing and is a perfect meal. The chickpea mixture in this lettuce wrap is full of flavor and ideal for sandwiches or topping a salad. It keeps extremely well in the refrigerator for take along meals. Try serving a scoop of this next to a leafy green salad.

GF **DF** **NF** **LS**

1 can (15.5 ounces, or 440 g) chickpeas, rinsed and drained (about 1½ cups, or 360 g)
2 tablespoons (28 ml) lemon juice
¼ cup (60 g) plain mayonnaise, any variety
3 chopped celery stalks
2 tablespoons (20 g) chopped white onions
¼ cup (15 g) chopped fresh parsley
2 tablespoons (12 g) chopped scallions
¼ teaspoon sea salt
¼ teaspoon ground black pepper
6 large romaine lettuce leaves, for serving

1. Add the chickpeas, lemon juice, mayonnaise, celery, onions, parsley, scallions, sea salt, and black pepper, in that order, to your blender container.

2. Pulse or blend on low until just combined and the chickpeas are mashed, but not smooth, using your tamper to help move the mixture along. This should be a thick and chunky mixture.

3. Add the chickpea salad to the lettuce leaves and roll them, using a toothpick to secure and place on a plate. If you rather not roll them in a leaf, serve them as an open face sandwich. Alternatively, you can add this to a bun or slices of fresh bread (omit for gluten-free option or use gluten-free products). Serve.

Southwest Veggie Burgers and Sliders

Makes twelve 3- to 4-inch (7.5 to 10 cm) round patties

While I like to serve these black bean corn cakes as a scrumptious vegetarian burger, they also make fabulous sliders or appetizers when made smaller and served with a dipping sauce of ranch dressing. Southwest flavors are bursting out of these versatile patties that I know will be a winner with your taste buds. These are hard to cook on an outdoor open flame grill but cook up perfectly on an oiled skillet.

GF **NF** **LS**

1 can (15 ounces, or 425 g) black beans, drained and rinsed, divided (about 1½ cups, or 360 g)
½ cup (about 82 g) corn, fresh or thawed from frozen
1 chopped red bell pepper, about 1 cup (150 g)
¾ cup (90 g) grated Cheddar cheese
¼ teaspoon garlic powder
¼ teaspoon paprika
1 teaspoon chile powder
½ teaspoon cumin
¼ teaspoon sea salt
2 whole eggs
1 cup (116 g) corn flour
2 tablespoons (28 ml) olive oil, for frying
Burger or slider buns, for serving (omit for gluten-free option or use gluten-free buns)

1. Set aside ½ cup (120 g) of black beans in a medium-size bowl with the fresh corn.

2. Add the remaining 1 cup (240 g) of black beans, bell pepper, cheddar cheese, garlic powder, paprika, chile powder, cumin, sea salt, eggs, and corn flour to your blender container.

3. Blend on medium until combined, but not completely smooth.

4. Transfer the mixture to the bowl with the black beans and corn and gently mix with a spatula to combine. Add more corn flour if the mixture is too runny.

5. Heat a skillet over medium-high heat. Add a generous amount of olive oil to the pan. For sliders, small burgers, or appetizer cakes, drop ¼-cup-size (60 ml) patties onto the skillet and cook them until golden brown on each side and hot in the center, about 4 minutes. If you want to make larger burgers to eat in a bun, drop ⅓-cup-size (80 ml) patties to the skillet and cook for 5 to 7 minutes.

Cheese and Olive Empanadas

Makes 12 empanadas

Empanadas are an easy finger food. They're great for parties, appetizers, and sports games. They aren't always easy to make, however, but this blender version is. To save on time, make the dough the night before and keep it in the refrigerator until ready to assemble and bake.

FOR THE EMPANADA DOUGH

3 whole eggs
1 cup (235 ml) safflower oil
1 cup (235 ml) 2% milk
1 cup (250 g) whole milk ricotta cheese
1½ teaspoons sea salt
3 cups (375 g) unbleached all-purpose flour

FOR THE EMPANADA FILLING

1 cup (115 g) shredded mozzarella cheese
½ cup (58 g) shredded Cheddar cheese
½ cup (50 g) chopped green olives

1. Preheat the oven 375°F (190°C, or gas mark 5).

2. Get your fillings ready. In a small bowl, mix the mozzarella and Cheddar cheese together with a spoon. Place the olives in another small bowl.

3. Add the eggs, safflower oil, milk, ricotta cheese, sea salt, and all-purpose flour to your blender container. Blend on medium until fully combined and smooth.

4. Fill a 12-cup muffin pan lightly sprayed with oil or lined with silicone baking cups one-quarter full to cover the bottom of each muffin cup.

5. Add 1 heaping tablespoon (7 g) of the shredded cheese mixture and then 1 teaspoon of the olives to each muffin cup. Then, fill the rest of each muffin cup ¾ full of batter to cover the filling.

6. Bake the empanadas 20 to 25 minutes until cooked through and the tops are golden.

Zucchini and Pea Fritters

Makes 16 fritters

These vegetable-rich fritters are full of zucchini and peas to help you get your daily servings of vegetables in for the day. Serve as a quick meal or a fantastic appetizer.

1 cup (120 g) chopped unpeeled zucchini, about 1 zucchini
1 cup (125 g) flour, any variety (use gluten-free for gluten-free option)
1 whole egg
½ cup (40 g) shredded Parmesan cheese
2 tablespoons (28 ml) olive oil
½ teaspoon sea salt
½ teaspoon ground black pepper
½ teaspoon dried parsley
½ cup (75 g) fresh peas or (65 g) thawed from frozen
Olive oil, for frying

1. Add the zucchini, flour, egg, Parmesan cheese, olive oil, sea salt, and black pepper to your blender container. Blend until combined.

2. Transfer the mixture to a medium-size bowl and add in the parsley and peas. Mix with a spatula to combine.

3. Heat a skillet with a generous coating of olive oil. Add round patties, about 1 tablespoon (15 ml) in size, to the skillet. Cook until brown and heated through, about 2 minutes on each side. Serve hot with a side of sour cream.

Beef and Vegetable Pie

Makes 1 pie, about 12 servings

This blender pie has been a staple recipe in my family for years. On special occasions, my mom would make this and we'd be chomping on leftovers for days. It's good served warm or cold.

FOR THE FILLING
¼ cup (40 g) chopped white onion
1 clove of garlic, minced
1½ pounds (680 g) ground beef
1 medium tomato, chopped
1 teaspoon sea salt
½ teaspoon ground black pepper
¾ cup (98 g) green peas, thawed from
   frozen

FOR THE PIE BATTER
1¾ cups (410 ml) milk, any variety
¾ cup (175 ml) safflower oil
5 whole eggs
½ tablespoon (8 g) sea salt
1 cup (100 g) grated Parmesan cheese
2½ cups (340 g) unbleached white flour

1. First, make the filling. Place a teaspoon of olive oil in a large pan. Add the onion. Cook until soft and translucent, about 5 minutes. Next, add the garlic, ground beef, tomato, sea salt, and black pepper.

2. Simmer until the beef is browned, cooked through, and all the juices have reduced. Remove from the heat and let cool. Add the

uncooked green peas to the pan and mix with a spoon, but do not cook.

3. Meanwhile, add the milk, oil, eggs, sea salt, and Parmesan cheese to your blender container.

4. Blend until smooth. While the motor is running on low to medium speed, slowly add the flour in batches, using the tamper or stopping to scrape down the sides with a spatula to redistribute the mixture, if needed. The dough should be the consistency of a heavy pancake batter. Depending on your eggs, the batter maybe too runny. If it is runny, add a tablespoon (9 g) of flour at the time until you get the right consistency.

5. Preheat the oven to 375°F (190°C, or gas mark 5). Lightly oil and flour a 10 x 13-inch (25 x 33 cm) ceramic or glass casserole dish.

6. Put a quarter of the batter in the pan. Spread the cooled filling over the top of the batter and then pour the rest of the batter over the filling, covering the filling.

7. Bake for 55 to 60 minutes or until set and browned on top. Remove from oven and let cool. Cut into rectangular portions.

VARIATION: This pie can be made with a variety of fillings to change up the flavor. Follow the same directions for the beef and vegetable filling, but substitute the ground beef with the same amount of shredded or ground chicken, ground pork, shrimp, or sautéed mushrooms. If you are using a vegetable-only mixture, be sure to sauté vegetables thoroughly or the extra water they have can ruin the pie.

12

VEGETABLE
SIDES

You might've never thought that you could make quick vegetable side dishes in your blender, but I've got good news, you can and you'll love it. You'll have gourmet accompaniments on the table in no time because your power blender can chop vegetables quickly and evenly for slaws, puree them nicely for relishes, and make delicious sauces to enhance a side.

◄ Classic Coleslaw

Makes 7 servings

Coleslaw is a picnic and summertime must-have alongside barbecue, chicken meals, or sandwiches. This version can be made very quickly if you are short on time and has a beautiful presentation.

1 small head of green cabbage, cored and cut into 5 or 6 small wedges
¼ cup (25 g) purple cabbage, cored and cut into small wedges
¼ cup (40 g) white onion, roughly chopped
¼ cup (33 g) carrots, roughly chopped
½ cup (115 g) mayonnaise
⅓ cup (115 g) honey
¼ cup (60 ml) milk, any variety
3 tablespoons (45 ml) lemon juice
1 tablespoon (15 ml) apple cider vinegar
½ teaspoon sea salt
¼ teaspoon ground black pepper

1. In batches, add the cabbage, only filling your blender container halfway full, about 1 or 2 wedges. Add enough water to cover the cabbage. Blend for a quick second on high until roughly chopped.

2. Transfer the cabbage and water to a colander to drain. Continue in batches until all the cabbage has been chopped. Put the drained cabbage in a large bowl.

3. Add the onion and carrot to your blender container. Blend until chopped, but do not overblend. Place the onion-and-carrot mixture into the bowl with the cabbage and mix to combine.

4. Add the mayonnaise, honey, milk, lemon juice, apple cider vinegar, sea salt, and black pepper to your blender container.

5. Blend until combined and smooth.

6. Add the dressing on top of the cabbage mixture in the bowl. Lightly toss with a large spoon. Serve immediately or cover and refrigerate to let flavors combine for at least 2 hours.

☞ BLENDING TIP

High-powered blenders can wet chop cabbage very well. If you've never tried this technique before, this recipe is a good one to start with. Always make sure the core is removed from the cabbage wedges before chopping. If the wedge will not chop, stop the machine. Break apart the wedge into a smaller piece to easily allow the blender to chop it.

Cranberry Orange Relish

Makes 1½ cups (365 g)

Perfect as a side to Thanksgiving meals, this relish is also so good alongside grilled chicken. It's also a great way to use cranberries when they are fresh and in season.

1 small peeled and quartered orange
3 cups (300 g) cranberries, fresh or thawed from frozen
¼ cup (36 g) coconut sugar
⅛ teaspoon sea salt
½ teaspoon grated orange rind

1. Add the orange, cranberries, coconut sugar, sea salt, and orange rind to your blender container.

2. Blend on low a few seconds until the cranberries are broken up and the mixture is combined, but not a smooth puree. Serve.

Carrot, Beet, and Apple Slaw

Makes 3 servings

A sweet, bright red slaw that is absolutely gorgeous on your plate, this side is healthy and satisfying. Your blender will make quick work of emulsifying the dressing which really brings out and balances the flavors of the slaw. Serve it with a protein such as fish or chicken or as a salad meal if you're eating light or on a cleanse.

FOR THE SLAW

1 cup (110 g) shredded raw carrot
1 cup (120 g) shredded raw beet
2 cups (170 g) shredded raw apple, any variety (I use Granny Smith.)
¼ cup (35 g) raisins

FOR THE DRESSING

¼ cup (60 ml) lemon juice
3 tablespoons (45 ml) olive oil
½ teaspoon sea salt

1. Place the carrots, beets, apples, and raisins in a medium-size bowl.

2. Add the lemon juice, orange juice, olive oil, and sea salt to your blender container. Blend until fully combined.

3. Pour the dressing mix on top of the slaw. Use a spoon to gently combine all ingredients. Serve.

Cheese and Chive Cauliflower Mash ▷

Makes 4 servings

This amazing side dish tastes just like mashed potatoes—maybe better. It's fabulous if you're on a low-carb diet, and I guarantee everyone will love the cheesy flavor. If you're into meal prepping, this is a great recipe to make ahead of time as an easy dinner side dish for a busy week.

GF NF LS

1 large cauliflower bunch, florets and stem, chopped into 1-inch (2.5 cm) chunks, about 6 cups (600 g)
4 ounces (115 g) softened cream cheese
¼ cup (25 g) grated Parmesan cheese
¼ cup (60 g) sour cream
1 cup (120 g) grated Cheddar cheese
½ teaspoon garlic powder
½ teaspoon sea salt
¼ teaspoon ground black pepper
2 tablespoons (1 g) dried chives

1. Cook the cauliflower in a large pot of boiling water until it is tender, about 10 to 15 minutes.

2. Meanwhile, combine the cream cheese, Parmesan cheese, sour cream, Cheddar cheese, garlic powder, sea salt, and black pepper to your blender container.

3. When the cauliflower is ready, drain it well and pat excess water off with a towel.

4. Add the cauliflower to the blender container with the other ingredients and blend until it is smooth. It's best if you do this in small batches.

5. Put the cauliflower mash into a serving bowl and add the dried chives. Mix with a spoon until combined. Serve.

Garlic Mashed Potatoes

Makes 6 servings

The perfect way to make mashed potatoes is in your blender, and it's easy to make this silky-smooth side dish with its assistance. Your hand will never get tired of mashing potatoes again, and you won't believe the creamy texture. This luxurious pan of potatoes has a hint of garlic, and it will quickly become the most popular side dish you offer your guests. If you don't do dairy, use vegan butter and nondairy milk as substitutes. I prefer gold potatoes but white potatoes taste delicious, too. Don't worry about peeling the potatoes perfectly, the blender will combine any extra peel pieces nicely.

6 gold or white potatoes (about 3 pounds or 1.4 kg), roughly peeled and cut into 1-inch (2.5 cm) cubes
4 cloves of garlic, minced
2 tablespoons (28 ml) olive oil
2 tablespoons (28 g) butter
¼ cup (60 ml) milk, any variety
1 teaspoon sea salt
½ teaspoon ground black pepper

1. Place the cubed potatoes in a large stockpot. Cover them with water and bring to a boil. Cook, uncovered, until firm but tender, about 15 to 20 minutes.

2. Meanwhile, add the garlic, olive oil, butter, milk, sea salt, and black pepper to your blender container.

3. With a spoon, transfer the cooked potatoes to your blender container.

4. Blend until well combined, smooth, and creamy, using the tamper or stopping to scrape down the sides with a spatula, about 1 minute. The blender will make them silky smooth, but if you prefer a chunkier side dish, don't blend them very long.

5. Add more garlic or sea salt, to taste. Serve.

Sweet Potato Mash

Makes 4 servings

This not-so-sweet version of creamy sweet potatoes are for those who prefer savory sides. Because the skins of sweet potatoes are hearty, be sure to peel them well. Boiling these potatoes instead of roasting ensures a silky texture without using a lot of oil, butter, or added liquid.

4 sweet potatoes (about 2 pounds or 1 kg), peeled and cut into 1-inch (2.5 cm) cubes
1 teaspoon sea salt
4 ounces (115 g) Neufchatel cheese

1. Place the sweet potatoes in a large stockpot. Cover them with water and bring to a boil. Cook until tender, about 20 minutes.

2. With a spoon, transfer the potatoes to your blender container. Add the sea salt and Neufchatel cheese.

3. Blend until well combined, smooth, and creamy, using the tamper to push the potatoes into the blades or stopping frequently to redistribute the mixture with a spatula. They are fully blended when they reach a whipped texture. Serve.

MAPLE SWEET POTATO MASH VARIATION: If you like a sweeter potato mash without dairy, use 2 tablespoons (28 g) of coconut oil plus 2 tablespoons (40 g) of maple syrup, in place of the Neufchatel cheese, to give it a hint of sweetness.

Salt-and-Pepper Cauliflower Rice

Makes 4 servings

Simple and extremely versatile, this riced cauliflower can be used in place of traditional rice in any dish for a more healthful meal. Think rice casseroles, rice bowls, homemade sushi, and side dishes. Made ahead of time, it keeps well for at least 3 days in the refrigerator.

V **GF** **DF** **NF** **LS**

1 cauliflower bunch, florets, chopped into 1-inch chunks (2.5 cm), about 4 cups (400 g)
½ teaspoon ground pink Himalayan sea salt
½ teaspoon ground black pepper

1. Add half of the chopped cauliflower to your blender container.

2. Blend on low to medium speed or pulse a few times, using the tamper or stopping to scrape down the sides until the cauliflower is "riced." Do not overblend or it will be mushy.

3. Transfer the mixture to a bowl, pull out any large florets that were not riced, and put them back into the blender. Continue 'ricing' the rest of the florets. If you don't have a tamper, it's best to do this in increments using 1 cup (100 g) of cauliflower at a time.

4. Add the sea salt and black pepper to the bowl of riced cauliflower. Gently mix with a spoon to combine.

5. Add more sea salt and black pepper to taste. Serve.

☞ **SERVING TIP**

Make a healthy and filling 'rice bowl' by adding cauliflower rice to a bowl and topping it with sautéed vegetables and grilled meat.

Sour Cream and Onion Kale Chips

Makes 2 to 4 servings

Baked kale chips are a great alternative to other chip options. This highly addictive dairy-free version is so good you can't just have one, which is totally fine because it's kale. You can use any variety of kale for these chips, but I find that lacinato, also called dinosaur kale, makes the best chip. Don't use baby kale, as it's light delicate texture never makes a good chip. It might take some experimenting to get this recipe right in your oven. Once you do, you'll be glad you did.

1 to 2 heads of lacinato kale
1 cup (140 g) cashews, soaked in water for 2 hours
½ cup (120 ml) water, plus more if needed
4 tablespoons (60 ml) fresh lemon juice
2 tablespoons (28 ml) raw apple cider vinegar
¼ teaspoon sea salt
3 tablespoons (30 g) finely minced shallots

1. Preheat the oven to 325°F (170°C, or gas mark 3).

2. Remove the stems from the kale leaves by using a knife or peeling them from the stem, starting from the bottom. Rip or cut them into 2- to 3-inch (5 to 7.5 cm) pieces. Rinse with water and dry thoroughly in a salad spinner to remove all moisture and place them in a medium-size bowl.

3. Add the soaked cashews, water, lemon juice, apple cider vinegar, and sea salt to your blender container.

4. Blend on high until completely combined and smooth. It should be the consistency of a salad dressing. Add more water, 2 tablespoons (28 ml) at a time, if necessary, to blend. It is important that the cashews are fully blended and the sauce is not too gritty.

5. Add the shallots and pulse once to gently mix within the mixture, but not fully blended.

6. Pour the sauce onto the kale chips. Toss the mixture with a spoon until evenly coated and then use your hands to ensure that the mixture is evenly distributed on the kale.

7. Transfer the coated chips to 1 or 2 silicone mat–lined baking sheets. Be sure they are in a single layer for crispiness and even cooking.

8. Bake for 20 minutes, remove from the oven, and flip the chips.

9. Bake for another 10 to 15 minutes until cooked and many are crispy, watching closely to make sure they don't burn. Serve. These chips don't keep well when stored.

13

MUFFINS, PANCAKES, AND OTHER QUICK BREADS

Whether you're starting the day short on time or you want to enjoy a nice weekend brunch with company, breakfast is a great time to use your blender because it makes everything easy. Think savory egg dishes, sweet muffins, and scrumptious breads made instantaneously by using only a few kitchen tools. Enjoy these delightful ways to start your day—many of which double as a snack, dessert, or accompaniment to a main meal.

 DF NF

1 cup (235 ml) rice or almond milk (omit for nut-free option)
1 whole egg
½ cup (125 g) unsweetened applesauce
½ cup (100 g) sugar or (72 g) coconut sugar
¼ cup (60 ml) melted coconut oil
½ cup (60 g) white whole wheat flour
1 cup (96 g) gluten-free old-fashioned rolled oats
1 teaspoon vanilla extract
1 teaspoon cinnamon plus extra for dusting
1½ teaspoons baking powder
½ teaspoon baking soda
½ teaspoon sea salt
½ cup (75 g) raisins

1. Preheat the oven to 400°F (200°C, or gas mark 6).

2. Add the almond milk, egg, applesauce, sugar, coconut oil, wheat flour, rolled oats, vanilla, cinnamon, baking powder, baking soda, and sea salt to your blender container.

3. Blend until combined and smooth but do not overblend. Add in the raisins and mix with a spatula to combine.

4. Spoon or pour into a 12-cup muffin pan lightly sprayed with oil or lined with silicone baking cups about ⅔ full. Dust the top of each muffin with a pinch of extra cinnamon.

5. Bake for 15 minutes or until lightly brown on top. Let the muffins cool for 5 minutes before removing from the pan.

▲ Cinnamon Raisin Oatmeal Muffins

Makes 12 muffins

This ultimate blender muffin is made in a flash, and it is perfect for meal prepping ahead of time. There is no easier weekday breakfast or snack. Bonus: It's heart-healthy and perfect if you're trying to control cholesterol. Serve them with jelly or a lightly whipped honey butter.

Chocolate Coconut Protein Muffins ▷

Makes 12 muffins

These muffins are the perfect breakfast or snack. My good friend, Amy, is a great baker and passed this amazing recipe down to me. They are packed with protein and heart-healthy fiber, and they have an extremely moist texture. There's no need to use oat flour—the beauty of your blender is that it will pulverize rolled oats into flour, already saving you a step.

GF **NF**

1 cup (235 ml) egg whites
1 whole egg
½ cup (115 g) cottage cheese
¼ cup (50 g) sugar or (36 g) coconut sugar
2 tablespoons (16 g) powdered stevia
1½ cups (144 g) gluten-free old-fashioned
 oats
½ teaspoon baking powder
¼ teaspoon sea salt
2 tablespoons (16 g) vanilla protein powder
1 tablespoon (5 g) cocoa powder
1 teaspoon coconut extract
½ cup (30 g) unsweetened coconut flakes
¼ cup (44 g) mini chocolate chips

1. Preheat the oven to 350°F (180°C, or gas mark 4).

2. Add the egg whites, eggs, cottage cheese, sugar, powdered stevia, oats, baking powder, sea salt, vanilla protein powder, cocoa powder, and coconut extract to your blender container.

3. Blend until completely combined, smooth, and the oats have blended thoroughly—but do not overblend.

4. Remove your blender container from the base and add in the coconut flakes. Use a spoon to gently mix them in the batter.

5. Pour or use a small ladle to scoop spoonfuls of the batter into a 12-cup muffin pan lightly sprayed with oil or lined with silicone baking cups. Top each muffin with a few chocolate chips.

6. Bake for 20 to 22 minutes until the tops are lightly golden brown. Let the muffins cool for 5 minutes before removing from the pan.

Vegan Orange Marmalade Muffins

Makes 12 muffins

After making these muffins, I gave some to my father who would normally not eat a vegan cupcake. To my delight, he ate them and loved them—proof for me that this recipe was a winner. It doesn't matter if you are a vegan or not, these moist and deliciously orange treats are something you'll love to wake up to for breakfast.

¾ cup (175 ml) orange juice
½ cup (150 g) orange marmalade
⅓ cup (80 ml) safflower or grapeseed oil
¼ cup (80 g) maple syrup
1 teaspoon orange zest
2 cups (240 g) whole wheat pastry flour
1 teaspoon baking powder
1 teaspoon baking soda
½ teaspoon sea salt

1. Preheat the oven to 350°F (180°C, or gas mark 4).

2. Add the orange juice, marmalade, oil, maple syrup, and orange zest to your blender container.

3. Blend until completely combined and smooth.

4. In a large bowl, add the flour, baking powder, baking soda, and sea salt together until well combined. Pour the liquid mixture to this bowl and using a large spoon, stir to combine, but do not overmix.

5. Pour or use a small ladle to scoop spoonfuls of the batter into a 12-cup muffin pan lightly sprayed with oil or lined with silicone baking cups.

6. Bake for 20 to 25 minutes until the tops are lightly golden brown. Let the muffins cool for 5 minutes before removing from the pan.

Cheddar Biscuits

Makes 9 biscuits

Do you love Cheddar biscuits? Me too. This gluten-free, low-carb version made with almond flour tastes so good, you'll never go back to the regular ones. Consider adding chopped jalapeños, garlic powder, chopped sun-dried tomatoes, or spices of your choice to change up the flavor. Serve these for breakfast with butter or alongside soup and salad.

GF **LS**

2 whole eggs
⅓ cup (77 g) plain Greek yogurt
4 tablespoons (60 ml) melted butter or coconut oil
1½ cups (168 g) almond flour
¼ teaspoon sea salt
1 tablespoon (14 g) baking powder
½ cup (60 g) grated Cheddar cheese

1. Preheat the oven to 400°F (200°C, or gas mark 6).

2. Add the eggs, Greek yogurt, butter, almond flour, sea salt, baking powder, and Cheddar cheese to your blender container.

3. Blend on low until combined, using the tamper and stopping frequently to scrape down the sides. The dough will be thick and fluffy.

4. Using a spoon or small ladle, scoop the mixture evenly into 9 paper or silicone lined muffin cups. Alternatively, using a 1 or 2 tablespoon (15 to 28 ml) measure, drop the batter a few inches (7.5 cm) apart onto a silicone baking mat or parchment paper–lined baking sheet.

5. Bake for 10 to 12 minutes or until golden on top.

Classic Crepes

Makes 10 servings

If you want to make a gourmet brunch or meal in a flash, this quick and fresh recipe is a good choice. Crepes can be stuffed with an array of wonderful ingredients to make them an amazing meal any time of day. Try them stuffed with fresh fruit or baked fruit compote. Apples, peaches, blueberries, cherries, strawberries, and ricotta cheese with chocolate chips are some of my favorites. If you're into savory crepes, chopped asparagus, mushrooms, and cheese are a fabulous choice to fill these with.

2 whole eggs
½ cup (120 ml) milk or almond milk (omit for nut-free option)
½ cup (120 ml) water
1 cup (136 g) unbleached all-purpose flour
¼ teaspoon sea salt
2 tablespoons (28 g) softened unsalted grass-fed butter

1. Add the eggs, milk, water, flour, and sea salt to your blender container.

2. Blend on low until just combined. Add the butter and process again until combined.

3. Heat a lightly oiled crepe pan or skillet over medium heat. Scoop approximately ¼ cup (60 ml) of mixture onto the pan and tilt the pan in a circular motion to evenly coat the bottom with thin layer of the batter.

4. Cook for 2 minutes or until the bottom is lightly brown and the top develops bubbles. Loosen the crepe with a spatula and flip it to cook the other side.

5. Cook for 1 to 2 minutes until lightly brown and cooked through.

6. Transfer the crepe onto a plate and roll or fold with your favorite filling. Repeat with the remaining batter.

VARIATION: To make these gluten-free, use a 1 to 1 gluten-free all-purpose flour mix in place of the all-purpose flour in this recipe.

Blueberry Pancakes

Makes 10 pancakes

Once I made my husband wild blueberry muffins and overmixed the batter. The blueberries turned the batter very blue. When he bit into it, I never saw him laugh so hard at the smurf-blue color it became. These are similar to those muffins in that they taste fantastic but they incorporate blueberries into the actual batter and they are also added in, so the entire pancake is a beautiful blue-ish hue. You'll love that these are made quickly in your blender and are very moist.

NF

1 cup (235 ml) 2% milk
1 whole egg
1½ cups (220 g) fresh blueberries, divided
1½ cups (204 g) unbleached all-purpose flour
2 tablespoons (18 g) coconut sugar
1 teaspoons baking powder
½ teaspoon sea salt
Butter or coconut oil, for frying
Maple syrup and fresh berries, for serving

1. Add the milk, egg, 1 cup (145 g) of blueberries, all-purpose flour, coconut sugar, baking powder, and sea salt to your blender container.

2. Blend until combined and smooth, but do not overblend. Add the remaining ½ cup (75 g) of blueberries to the container and gently stir with a spatula to combine.

3. Add butter or coconut oil to a skillet or griddle over medium-high heat.

4. Using a ladle, scoop ¼ cup (60 ml) of the batter onto the skillet for each pancake. Cook for 2 to 3 minutes on each side or until golden brown and cooked through.

5. Serve with maple syrup and berries.

Gluten-Free Pancakes

Makes 6 pancakes

Do you love pancakes but don't do gluten? This easy gluten-free version can be whipped up with dry rice you have in your pantry. These are best enjoyed fresh.

GF **NF**

1 cup (185 g) uncooked dry white rice
¼ cup (30 g) tapioca flour
2 teaspoons baking powder
⅛ teaspoon sea salt
½ cup (120 ml) milk, any variety
2 tablespoons (40 g) maple syrup
1 tablespoon (14 g) softened grass-fed butter
1 whole egg
⅛ teaspoon cinnamon
Butter or oil, for frying and serving
Maple syrup and fresh berries, for serving

1. Add the dry white rice to your blender container. Blend on high until it becomes a fine powder.

2. Add the tapioca flour, baking powder, sea salt, milk, maple syrup, butter, egg, and cinnamon to your blender container.

3. Blend on high until very smooth. The batter will be fairly thin.

4. Add butter or coconut oil to a skillet or griddle over medium-high heat.

5. Using a ladle, scoop ¼ cup (60 ml) of the batter onto the skillet for each pancake. Cook for 1 to 2 minutes on each side or until golden brown and cooked through.

6. Serve with maple syrup, butter, and berries.

Whole Wheat Waffles ▶

Makes about 5 cups (1.1 L) of batter

We use applesauce to eliminate oil in these low-fat, whole-grain waffles that are soft on the inside and lightly crispy on the outside. Dress them up with chopped fresh fruit, thick maple syrup, or even some Coconut Whipped Cream (page 250).

NF

2 whole eggs
½ cup (125 g) applesauce
1¾ cups (410 ml) 1% milk or any nondairy
  milk (use nut-free for nut-free option)
½ teaspoon vanilla extract
2 cups (250 g) whole wheat flour
4 teaspoons (18 g) baking powder
¼ teaspoon sea salt
Fresh peaches or nectarines
Maple syrup
Coconut Whipped Cream (page 250;
  optional)

1. Preheat your waffle iron.

2. Add the eggs, applesauce, milk, vanilla, flour, baking powder, and sea salt to your blender container.

3. Blend until just combined and smooth, but do not overmix.

4. Spray the waffle iron lightly with oil. Pour the batter into the waffle iron, close, and cook until golden brown and crisp according to your waffle irons manufacturer's instructions.

5. Serve with fresh peaches, maple syrup, and the Coconut Whipped Cream (if using).

◄ Gluten-Free Citrus Pound Cake

Makes 1 loaf, 16 slices

I don't make many baked goods, but this pound cake is hands down one of my favorites in this category. Everyone loves it, every time! If you have guests coming over and you want to make a sweet treat that is gluten-free, this is your recipe. It only takes minutes to whip up. Its texture is perfect, and it makes the best breakfast or dessert. It freezes well, so it's great to keep on hand in your freezer for a rainy day. I use Swerve sweetener to make this sugar-free. Feel free to use sugar or any safe sweetener such as monk fruit, coconut sugar, stevia, or erythritol.

GF **LS**

½ cup (112 g) unsalted melted butter
8 ounces (225 g) softened cream cheese
1½ cups (300 g) granular sweetener of choice such as sugar (omit for low-sugar option), erythritol, or Swerve sweetener
8 whole eggs
1 teaspoon vanilla extract
½ teaspoon lemon extract
½ teaspoon orange extract
2½ cups (280 g) almond flour
1½ teaspoons baking powder
½ teaspoon sea salt

1. Preheat the oven to 350°F (180°C, or gas mark 4).

2. Add the butter, cream cheese, and sweetener to your blender container. Blend until smooth.

3. Add in the eggs, vanilla, lemon extract, and orange extract. Blend until these are well combined.

4. In a medium-size bowl, mix together the almond flour, baking powder, and sea salt.

5. Add the liquid mixture from your blender to the bowl and mix with a spatula until well combined.

6. Pour the batter into a 8 x 4-inch (20 x 10 cm) loaf pan lightly sprayed with oil. Bake for 70 minutes or until a toothpick inserted in the center comes out clean.

☞ **SERVING TIP**

This pound cake is wonderful on its own, but the batter can easily be made into many different desserts. Add strawberries and whipped cream on top or glaze it with a chocolate drizzle. You can also bake this batter in a Bundt pan. When cooled, spread icing on it and add sprinkles for a beautiful birthday cake.

Broccoli and Cheese Frittata

Makes one 8-inch (20 cm) frittata, about 6 servings

I love eggs. I love it even more that you can make great egg dishes in your blender—quickly without having to whisk. This frittata is good any time of day, but I usually serve it for breakfast.

4 whole eggs
¼ cup (60 ml) milk, any variety
¼ teaspoon sea salt
⅛ teaspoon ground black pepper
½ cup (60 g) grated Cheddar cheese
1 cup (91 g) finely chopped broccoli florets
Butter or olive oil, for frying

1. Add the eggs, milk, sea salt, and black pepper to your blender container. Blend quickly on low for a few seconds until combined. Do not overblend this mixture.

2. Remove the blender container from the base.

3. Add the Cheddar cheese and broccoli and mix them in with a spatula to quickly combine.

4. Heat an omelet pan or 8-inch (20 cm) round skillet on the stove.

5. Add the butter or olive oil. Once melted, pour the frittata mixture into the skillet.

6. Cook over low to medium heat until eggs are set, about 5 to 7 minutes.

7. Remove from the heat and cover. Let sit 5 to 10 minutes or until no visible liquid remains.

Vanilla Coconut Rice Cereal

Makes 2½ cups (415 g)

If you want a quick warm breakfast and have some dry rice in your kitchen, this is a great gluten-free option. Spice up your bowl by topping it with fresh blueberries, chopped strawberries, chopped dried apricots, raisins, dried cranberries, or nuts.

1 cup (185 g) dry uncooked white rice
2½ cups (570 ml) water
1 teaspoon vanilla bean paste
⅛ teaspoon sea salt
2 tablespoons (8 g) unsweetened coconut flakes
2 tablespoons (40 g) maple syrup

1. Add the dry rice to your blender container. Blend on high to create a cracked rice or for a smoother cereal, grind until it becomes a finer powder.

2. Transfer the rice to a small saucepan.

3. Add the water. Bring to a boil, whisking constantly. Reduce the heat to low and cover. Simmer until cooked, about 10 minutes.

4. Add the vanilla bean paste, sea salt, coconut flakes, and maple syrup. Stir to combine.

5. Serve hot with toppings of your choice.

VARIATION: For a nuttier hearty cereal, use brown rice in place of white rice. It will take slightly longer to cook.

Buttermilk Seed Bread

Makes 2 loaves, 28 servings

This bread is great to slice for sandwiches or for buttering up to accompany any meal. You'll love the pretty seeds poking through the loaf to give it texture and flavor.

NF

¾ cups (175 ml) warm water, 110°F (43°C)
1 tablespoon (12 g) active dry yeast
3 tablespoons (60 g) honey
2 cups (240 g) whole wheat flour
4 cups (500 g) white whole wheat flour
2 tablespoons (16 g) sesame seeds
2 tablespoons (24 g) flaxseeds
2 tablespoons (18 g) poppy seeds
2 teaspoons (10 g) sea salt
1½ cups (355 ml) buttermilk
2 tablespoons (28 g) butter, melted

1. Add the water, yeast, and honey to your blender container. Blend for 1 second until combined. Let it proof for 5 to 10 minutes.

2. Meanwhile, in a large bowl, combine the wheat flours, seeds, and sea salt. Gently mix with a spoon.

3. Add the butter and buttermilk to the blender container. Blend gently to combine.

4. Add the flour mixture to the blender container, ¼ cup (55 g) at a time, and blend gently to mix. When incorporated, pulse gently 6 to 8 times until a dough ball forms.

5. Remove the dough and place it in a well-oiled bowl. Turn it several times to coat the outside of the loaf. Cover with a damp cloth and let it sit until it doubles in size, about 45 minutes.

6. Punch down the dough. Divide the dough into 2 even loaves and place them in 2 well-oiled 9 x 5-inch (23 x 13 cm) loaf pans. Allow to rise until dough is doubled in size.

7. Bake at 375°F (190°C, or gas mark 5) for 25 to 30 minutes.

Apple Cranberry Oat Bake

Makes 8 servings

Great for a group of guests, this baked oatmeal dish is a crowd pleaser. It's a smooth, cake-like oatmeal bake that is easy to whip up quickly and perfect for brunch.

GF **NF**

1½ cups (355 ml) milk, almond milk (omit for nut-free option), or coconut milk
⅓ cup (107 g) maple syrup or (115 g) honey
2 whole eggs
3 tablespoons (42 g) melted unsalted grass-fed butter or coconut oil
2 teaspoons vanilla extract
2 teaspoons ground cinnamon
1 teaspoon baking powder
½ teaspoon sea salt
¼ teaspoon ground nutmeg
2 cups (192 g) gluten-free old-fashioned oats, divided
2½ cups (375 g) peeled and finely diced Granny Smith apples
¼ cup (30 g) dried cranberries
Grass-fed butter and maple syrup, for serving

1. Preheat the oven to 375°F (190°C, or gas mark 5).

2. Add the milk, maple syrup, eggs, butter, vanilla, cinnamon, baking powder, sea salt, and nutmeg to your blender container.

3. Blend on medium-high speed until well combined.

4. Add 1½ cups (144 g) of the oats. Blend until the mixture is fully combined.

5. Remove the blender container from the base and add in the remaining ½ cup (48 g) of oats. Gently mix with a spoon to combine.

6. Lightly spray an 8 x 8-inch (20 x 20-cm) baking dish with oil. Add the apples and dried cranberries to the bottom of the dish. Pour the oat mixture over the fruit. Bake for 42 to 45 minutes until lightly brown on top.

7. Serve warm with butter and maple syrup.

Gluten-Free Banana Bread ▶

Makes 1 loaf

Moist and delicious, this sweet bread is perfect for a quick breakfast along with a side of fruit. This recipe is low in sugar, but if you want to eliminate it, it's still good and naturally sweet without any extra. It's a perfect way to use up any ripe bananas you have around.

GF **DF**

3 whole eggs
¼ cup (60 ml) safflower oil
3 medium bananas, peeled and broken
  in chunks
2 cups (224 g) almond flour
1 teaspoon baking soda
¼ teaspoon sea salt
¼ cup (50 g) sugar or (36 g) coconut sugar

1. Preheat the oven to 350°F (180°C, or gas mark 4).

2. Add the eggs, safflower oil, bananas, almond flour, baking soda, sea salt, and sugar, in that order, to your blender container.

3. Blend until completely combined and smooth, about 10 seconds. Use the spatula and tamper to help evenly distribute the mixture to avoid overblending.

4. Pour into an 8 x 4-inch (20 x 10 cm) loaf pan lightly sprayed with coconut oil. Bake for 55 to 60 minutes or until a toothpick inserted in the center comes out clean.

5. Cool in the pan for 10 minutes and then transfer to a wire rack. Serve warm or at room temperature.

Banana Walnut Bread

Makes 1 loaf, about 16 slices

Moist and delicious, this will be a hit alongside coffee and tea for a quick breakfast.

3 ripe bananas, peeled and chopped, about 1½ cups (225 g)
¼ cup (60 g) plain yogurt
2 whole eggs
6 tablespoons (90 ml) melted unsalted butter
1 teaspoon vanilla extract
¼ teaspoon baking soda
½ teaspoon sea salt
¾ cup (150 g) sugar
1 cup (125 g) all-purpose flour
1 cup (128 g) whole wheat flour
1 cup (120 g) chopped walnuts (optional)

1. Preheat the oven to 350°F (180°C, or gas mark 4).

2. Add the bananas, yogurt, eggs, butter, vanilla, baking soda, and sea salt to your blender container.

3. Blend until completely combined and smooth.

4. Add the sugar and blend again until combined, just a few seconds.

5. In a medium-size bowl, gently mix the all-purpose flour and wheat flour.

6. Add the liquid mixture from your blender to the bowl and mix with a spatula until well combined. Be careful to not overmix or the bread will be dense.

7. Add the walnuts (if using) and use a spatula to gently combine.

8. Pour into an 8 x 4-inch (20 x 10 cm) loaf pan lightly sprayed with coconut oil. Bake for 50 to 55 minutes or until a toothpick inserted in the center comes out clean.

9. Cool in the pan for 10 minutes and then transfer to a wire rack. Serve warm or at room temperature.

Creamy Cornbread Cake

Makes 1 pan, 9 servings

This cornbread cake has a creamy, custard-like center that is heavenly served on its own or to accompany a meal.

NF

4 cups (950 ml) 2% milk
4 whole eggs
2 tablespoons (28 g) softened butter
3 cups (600 g) sugar
1½ cups (210 g) organic cornmeal, home-made or store-bought
2 tablespoons (16 g) unbleached all-purpose flour
1 tablespoon (14 g) baking powder
1 cup (100 g) grated Parmesan cheese

1. Preheat the oven to 350°F (180°C, or gas mark 4). Spray an 8 x 10-inch (20 x 25 cm) glass or ceramic baking dish with oil.

2. Add the milk, eggs, butter, sugar, cornmeal, flour, baking powder, and Parmesan cheese to your blender container.

3. Blend until completely smooth and blended, stopping to scrape down the sides with a spatula, if necessary. Try not to overblend. The batter will be very thin.

4. Pour the batter into the baking dish and use a spatula to even out the mixture.

5. Bake for 35 to 45 minutes or until a toothpick in the center comes out clean.

6. Cool on the counter at least 10 minutes before cutting and serving.

Quinoa Flatbread Pita

Makes 8 flatbread pitas

Quinoa is gluten-free, high in amino acids, rich in fiber, and easy to digest. Use these nutty flatbreads as a healthy alternative to a traditional pita or top it for a flatbread meal. They are dense and will keep you full, making it a great meal.

V **GF** **DF** **NF** **LS**

2 cups (346 g) whole dry white quinoa
¾ cup (143 g) dry uncooked brown rice
1 teaspoon sea salt
1 teaspoon olive oil
2 cups plus 2 tablespoons (505 ml) water
Olive oil, for frying

1. Add the brown rice to your blender container. Blend on high until you reach a fine powder. Transfer the flour to a bowl.

2. Add the dry quinoa to the blender container. Blend on high until you reach a fine powder. Add the brown rice back into the blender container.

3. Add the water, olive oil, and sea salt to the blender container.

4. Blend on medium speed until it is smooth and forms a thick dough. It should be the consistency of a thick pancake batter. If it's too thick, add more water, 1 to 2 tablespoons (12 to 28 ml) at a time.

5. Heat a nonstick skillet on medium-high heat.

6. Using a ladle or spoon, scoop about ½ cup (120 ml) of batter onto a generously oiled nonstick skillet.

7. Cook for 3 minutes on each side until lightly brown and cooked through.

☞ **SERVING TIP**

The list of flatbread meals you can create with this bread is endless. Try avocado and chicken topped with the Cucumber Ranch Dressing (page 155). Make a pizza flatbread by topping it with tomato sauce and mozzarella cheese or try a lighter meal with toppings of pear, blue cheese, and arugula.

▲ Honey Whole Wheat Bread

Makes 2 loaves, 28 servings

While making homemade bread is time consuming, you won't regret it once you taste it. Your blender will help you mix the dough. Wide-bottomed blender containers work best for recipes like this, if you have one. If you aren't using this right away, freeze it for later use. Because homemade bread has no preservatives, it will only stay fresh for a few days.

2 cups (475 ml) warm water, 110°F (43°C)
1 tablespoon (12 g) active dry yeast
½ cup (170 g) honey
3 cups (360 g) organic whole wheat flour
4 cups (500 g) organic white whole wheat flour
1½ teaspoons salt
⅓ cup (82 g) applesauce

1. Add the water, yeast, and honey to your blender container. Blend for 1 second until combined. Let it proof for 5 to 10 minutes.

2. Meanwhile, in a large bowl, combine the wheat flours and sea salt. Gently mix with a spoon.

3. Add the applesauce and the flour mixture to the blender container, ¼ cup (30 g) of flour at a time, and blend gently to mix.

4. When incorporated, pulse gently 6 to 8 times until a dough ball forms. If it becomes to hard to blend, transfer the mixture to a bowl and knead a few times.

5. Remove the dough and place it in a well-oiled bowl. Turn it several times to coat the outside of the loaf. Cover with a damp cloth and let it sit until it doubles in size, about 45 minutes.s

6. Punch down the dough. Divide the dough into two even loaves and place them in two well-oiled 9 x 5-inch (23 x 13 cm) loaf pans. Allow to rise until the dough has doubled in size.

7. Bake for 375°F (190°C, or gas mark 5) for 25 to 30 minutes.

Condensed Milk Sweet Bread ▶

Makes 2 large loaves or 29 small round rolls

This sweet quick bread uses the rich flavor of sweetened condensed milk to create an exclusive texture and taste. It's a uniquely Brazilian recipe that comes down from my mom and is always a hit for breakfast or to accompany a meal. You'll love that it doesn't need kneading.

NF **LS**

1 can (14 ounces, or 390 ml) sweetened condensed milk
2¼ cups (535 ml) warm water, 110°F (43°C)
⅔ cup (160 ml) safflower oil
2 tablespoons (28 g) room temperature melted butter
1 teaspoon sea salt
2 whole eggs
4½ teaspoons (about 18 g) Rapid Rise Yeast or Active Dry Yeast
8 cups (1 kg) unbleached all-purpose flour
Melted butter, for brushing bread

1. Add the condensed milk, water, oil, butter, sea salt, eggs, and yeast to your blender container.

2. Blend for a few seconds until well combined.

3. Put the flour in a large bowl. Transfer the liquid blender mixture to the bowl.

4. Using a spatula, mix the flour into the liquid until it forms a dough. Alternatively, you can transfer the contents to a board or

counter and gently mix with your hands until a dough is formed.

5. Shape the bread into rolls, a loaf, a braid, or any way you prefer. If you shape the dough into rolls, be sure to form them the same size to ensure even baking.

6. Place the dough in a warm spot for about 50 minutes to rise until doubled in size.

7. Brush the bread with melted butter just before baking.

8. Bake at 425°F (220°C, or gas mark 7) for 25 to 30 minutes until golden brown and a toothpick inserted in the center comes out clean.

Pao de Queso Cheese Rolls

Makes 12 rolls

You might have seen these gluten-free cheesy bread bites that are chewy on the inside and crispy on the outside sold at the grocery store in recent years. I've had them my entire life and consider myself lucky for it. *Pao de queso* is a cheese bread, usually formed into small round rolls. They accompany a dinner entree or are served as a snack. They are simply amazing, and I couldn't live my life without them. They originated in Brazil but are getting super popular worldwide because they are gluten-free. This recipe is courtesy of my Brazilian-born mom, so you know it's authentically good! These are best served warm, the day they are made.

GF **NF** **LS**

1 cup (235 ml) whole milk
½ cup (120 ml) grapeseed oil
1 teaspoon sea salt
3 whole eggs
3 cups (360 g) tapioca flour, also known as tapioca starch
1 cup (100 g) grated Parmesan cheese

1. Preheat the oven to 475°F (250°C, or gas mark 9). Lightly spray a 12-cup muffin pan with oil or line with silicone baking cups.

2. Add the milk, oil, sea salt, and eggs to your blender container. Blend on medium-high until fully combined.

3. Add the flour, a little at the time, blending in between additions. Tapioca flour is very fine, so add it carefully or your kitchen will easily be coated in flour.

4. Once the batter is well combined, add the Parmesan cheese. Pulse it quickly to mix the cheese into the batter, but do not overblend. The batter will be very thin.

5. Fill the 12-cup muffin pan evenly with the batter.

6. Bake for 20 minutes until the rolls rise and are crispy and slightly golden on the outside. Be careful not to overbake this bread.

7. Remove from oven and let cool for at least 5 minutes. Remove to a cooling rack before serving.

VARIATIONS

Smaller rolls: Divide the batter evenly among a mini muffin pan that yields 24. Follow the same baking instructions as above and bake for 10 to 12 minutes or until slightly golden.

Stuffed Pao De Queso: Divide the batter evenly among small ramekins and then split them in the middle and add your favorite filling, such as tuna fish, ham and cheese, or chopped olives. Follow the same baking instructions as above.

14

DESSERTS FROM THE
BLENDER

Your blender is the perfect choice for making creamy pies, rich puddings, and luxurious cheesecakes. It can pulverize the mixtures into the perfect texture—no lumps are ever left behind like they might be with stand mixers or food processors. Your blender also does a fabulous job of making gluten-free nut flour or coconut-based crusts in only minutes. Enjoy these healthful and seemingly sinful desserts, with little prep time and zero guilt.

▲ Chocolate Coconut Oat Balls

Makes 22 balls

A great snack or dessert, these oat balls are pure delight. They look like fudge truffles and make a beautiful presentation. I find them to be the perfect sweet treat after a yoga session.

1 cup (96 g) gluten-free old-fashioned rolled oats
2 tablespoons (14 g) ground flaxseed
1 tablespoon (5 g) cocoa powder
½ cup (130 g) almond butter
1 teaspoon vanilla extract
¼ cup (60 ml) water
2 tablespoons (40 g) honey
½ cup (30 g) unsweetened shredded coconut
¼ cup (44 g) dark chocolate chips
Cocoa powder and shredded coconut, for rolling

1. Place the oats in your blender and pulse until it turns into a flour.

2. Add the ground flaxseed, cocoa powder, almond butter, vanilla, water, honey, and shredded coconut to the container.

3. Pulse to get the mixture moving and then blend until combined, stopping to scrape down the sides.

4. The mixture will be warm, so let it chill before adding in the dark chocolate chips. Once cool, add the chocolate chips to the blender container. Use a spatula to mix the chips into the batter mixture.

5. Using a ½ tablespoon measure, shape into balls using your hands. Roll in cocoa powder or flaked coconut.

6. Transfer the balls to the refrigerator to chill for at least 30 minutes or until ready to serve.

Vanilla Chia Pudding

Makes 4 servings

If you like the idea of chia pudding but don't like the texture of the seeds, try this silky-smooth version. And if you're into dessert for breakfast, this one is for you. This vanilla infused pudding is a great dessert all on its own but is enhanced in a bowl layered with toppings like banana slices, coconut flakes, or fresh, chopped fruit. Black chia seeds work just fine for this recipe but the white variety makes for a better presentation.

2 cups (475 ml) rice milk
6 tablespoons (78 g) white chia seeds
1 tablespoon (15 ml) vanilla extract
2 tablespoons (40 g) honey or agave

1. Add the almond milk, chia seeds, vanilla, and honey or agave to your blender container.

2. Blend until smooth and combined and the chia have been pulverized.

3. Pour the pudding into an airtight glass container. Let it sit for 4 to 6 hours or overnight in the refrigerator to thicken. Serve.

VARIATION: Other nondairy milks work great in this recipe, too. Try using coconut milk or almond milk in place of the rice milk in this recipe.

Orange Mango Pudding ▶

Makes 2 servings

This will take you two minutes to whip up with ingredients you likely have already in your kitchen. It's a wonderfully smooth pudding that is full of vitamin C and sunshine. If you're on a cleanse or are looking for a quick low-fat dessert, this is the perfect pick garnished with coconut chips and white chia seeds.

1 large peeled and quartered orange
2 large peeled and pitted mangos
2 tablespoons (28 ml) coconut cream, taken from the top of a can of canned full-fat coconut milk

1. Place the orange, mango, and coconut cream in your blender container.

2. Blend on high until completely smooth and silky. This is best served immediately.

V GF DF NF

1½ cups (355 ml) full-fat canned coconut
   milk
½ tablespoon (8 ml) vanilla extract
1 cup (155 g) finely chopped fresh
   pineapple, rind removed, divided
1 tablespoon (20 g) honey or agave
¼ cup (52 g) chia seeds
2 tablespoons (8 g) unsweetened coconut
   flakes

1. Add the coconut milk, vanilla, ½ cup
(78 g) of pineapple, and honey or agave to
your blender container.

2. Blend until smooth and combined. Add the
chia seeds, remaining ½ cup (78 g) pineapple
and coconut flakes to the blender container
and use a spatula to gently combine.

3. Pour the pudding into an airtight glass
container and let it sit for 4 to 6 hours or
overnight in the refrigerator to thicken.

4. Make individual chia desserts by pouring
the mixture into ramekins instead of a large
bowl. Serve.

▲ Piña Colada Chia Pudding

Makes 4 servings

Just like a piña colada drink, this pudding's
flavor will whisk you away with its island-
esque flavors. It's rich, delicious, and
unbelievably dairy-free. You can use light
coconut milk, but I find the full-fat version
is much tastier and provides your body with
healthy fat.

Strawberry Yogurt Dip with Fruit Skewers ▶

Makes about 2 cups (450 g)

This yogurt dip is an ideal healthy dessert, and it also makes a great appetizer for any party. You might want to make this at the beginning of the week and leave it in the refrigerator for a quick sweet treat when you're feeling hungry. It's not only beautiful, but incredibly light and guilt-free.

GF **NF**

FOR THE DIP

2 cups (230 g) plain unsweetened 2% Greek yogurt
3 tablespoons (60 g) honey or agave
¼ cup (43 g) fresh chopped strawberries
1 teaspoon vanilla extract

FOR THE FRUIT SKEWERS

Wooden skewers
Chopped pineapple
Halved strawberries
Kiwi slices
Chopped apples
Green grapes

1. Place the Greek yogurt, honey or agave, strawberries, and vanilla into your blender container.

2. Blend until it's smooth and has a whipped-like texture. Taste and add more sweetener, if desired, and blend again.

3. Pour into a serving bowl and chill for at least 20 minutes to thicken.

4. Meanwhile, make fruit kabobs by sliding pineapple, strawberries, kiwi, apples, and green grapes onto wooden skewers.

5. To serve, place a bowl with the strawberry yogurt dip on a tray and arrange the skewers around it.

VARIATIONS

Blueberry Fruit Dip: Substitute the strawberries for ¼ cup (36 g) of fresh blueberries.

Chocolate Strawberry Fruit Dip: Add ¼ cup (20 g) of cocoa powder to the recipe ingredients.

V GF DF NF

¼ cup (60 ml) full-fat canned coconut milk
2 large avocados, peeled, pitted, and
    mashed (about 1½ cups or 345 g)
¼ cup (20 g) cocoa powder, unsweetened
2 teaspoons vanilla extract
¼ cup (80 g) maple syrup
2 pitted medjool dates

1. Place the coconut milk, mashed avocado, cocoa powder, vanilla, maple syrup, and dates in your blender container.

2. Blend until completely smooth and creamy, using the tamper or stopping to scrape down the sides, if needed.

3. Serve at room temperature or chilled.

▲ Raw Chocolate Pudding

Makes 2 servings

This pudding is silky smooth with no hint of an avocado taste. It's the perfect healthy dessert. The blender whips the mixture into a decadent mousse-like texture. To take this up a notch, top the pudding with fresh raspberries and unsweetened coconut flakes or layer in a glass jar with chopped fruit for a beautiful parfait.

Classic Pumpkin Pie ▶

Makes one 9-inch (23 cm) pie

Easy to make with just three main ingredients and a few spices, this will be your go-to holiday pie. It turns out great every time. I just love how I only have to wash one thing, my blender container, not a bowl and mixer, once this is done. It's the perfect blender-easy dessert recipe. While the pie is completely gluten-free, many store-bought crusts are not. There are a variety of pie crusts available, so be sure to use a gluten-free pie crust if you desire.

1 can (15 ounces or 425 g) pumpkin puree, store-bought or homemade (about 2 cups, or 490 g)

1 can (14 ounces, or 390 g) sweetened condensed milk (1¾ cups, or 410 ml)

2 whole eggs

¾ teaspoon ground cinnamon

½ teaspoon ground nutmeg

¼ teaspoon ground ginger

¼ teaspoon ground cloves

½ teaspoon sea salt

1 pie shell (9 inches, or 23 cm), store-bought or homemade, any variety (use gluten-free for gluten-free option)

Whipped cream (optional)

1. Preheat the oven to 425°F (220°C, or gas mark 7).

2. Add the pumpkin puree, sweetened condensed milk, egg, cinnamon, nutmeg, ginger, ground cloves, and sea salt to your blender container.

3. Blend on high until smooth, creamy, and completely combined. Pour the filling into the prepared pie shell.

4. Bake at 425°F (220°C, or gas mark 7) for 15 minutes. Then, reduce the temperature to 350°F (180°C, or gas mark 4) for 35 to 40 minutes until cooked through and slightly brown on top.

5. Let the pie cool completely at room temperature before topping with whipped cream (if desired) and serving. Store in the refrigerator.

☞ BLENDING TIP

If you'd like to make your own pumpkin puree instead of buying the canned version for recipes, it's easy to do. Simply place 2 cups (232 g) of cubed roasted fresh pumpkin, without the skin, plus ½ cup (120 ml) of water or low-sodium vegetable broth into your blender container. Blend on high for about a minute until smooth, using the tamper to press the pumpkin into the blades or stopping to scrape down the sides of the container with a spatula, if needed.

No-Bake Individual Cheesecakes

Makes 12 individual cheesecakes or one 9-inch (23 cm) round dish

Turn off your oven: it's not needed for this recipe! No one will know that this cheesecake is lower in fat and healthier than others out there, so don't tell. We're using thick Greek yogurt and low-fat cream cheese to make this a decadent, easy, and oven-free cheesecake. If you prefer to make a big pan of cheesecake, that works great too, but it will be a spoon dessert and not a sliceable cheesecake.

NF

FOR THE CRUST

1⅓ cup (about 112 g) graham cracker crumbs
4 tablespoons (60 ml) melted butter

FOR THE CHEESECAKE FILLING

4 packages (8 ounces, or 225 g, each) of softened low-fat cream cheese
2 cups (460 g) plain 0% Greek yogurt
½ cup (170 g) honey or (160 g) agave
¼ cup (60 ml) fresh lemon juice
2 tablespoons (28 ml) vanilla extract
¼ teaspoon sea salt
Fresh berries and lemon zest, for garnish

1. Add the graham cracker crumbs and butter to your blender container. Blend until combined and crumbly.

2. Using a spoon and your fingers, press the crust into the bottom of 3-inch (7.5 cm) ramekins or dessert bowls.

3. Rinse out your container. Add the cream cheese, Greek yogurt, honey, lemon juice, vanilla, and sea salt to your blender container. Make sure your cream cheese is softened or it will be harder to blend. Blend until smooth and well combined.

4. Using a ½ cup (120 ml) measure, pour the batter into the ramekins on top of the crust. Smooth out the top of each cheesecake with a spatula.

5. Cover the cheesecakes with plastic wrap and transfer it to a refrigerator to chill. Let sit for 3 hours or until set.

6. Garnish with berries and lemon zest. Serve.

NOTE: To make graham cracker crumbs, add store-bought or homemade graham crackers to your blender container. Blend on medium speed until it forms a flour and is crumbly.

VARIATION: To make this no-bake cheesecake gluten-free, replace the graham cracker crumbs with gluten-free graham crackers or almond flour.

Chunky Apple Cake Bars

Makes twelve 3-inch (7.5 cm) square pieces of cake

This apple cake is perfect for a dessert where you don't want something heavy, but just a little finger dessert. It makes a great accompaniment to coffee or tea time with friends.

DF **NF**

5 medium apples
2 tablespoons (28 ml) fresh lemon juice
2 cups (250 g) all-purpose flour
2 cups (400 g) sugar, divided
1 tablespoon (14 g) baking powder
2½ teaspoons (6 g) ground cinnamon
3 whole eggs
¾ cup (175 ml) safflower oil

1. Preheat the oven to 375°F (190°C, or gas mark 5). Lightly spray a 9 x 13-inch (23 x 33 cm) baking dish with oil.

2. Peel, core, and chop the apples in small to medium chunks, saving the peels in a bowl. In a medium-size bowl, place the chopped apples and coat them with lemon juice to prevent browning.

3. In another large size bowl, add the flour, baking powder, 1 cup (200 g) of sugar, chopped apples, and cinnamon. Mix with a spoon to combine.

4. Meanwhile, add the eggs, safflower oil, the remaining 1 cup (200 g) of sugar, and apple peels to your blender container. Blend well until the apple peels have fully combined.

5. Add the liquid blender mixture to the flour mixture in the bowl. With a spatula, mix gently until everything is thoroughly combined. Pour this mixture into your baking pan.

6. Bake for about 25 to 30 minutes until golden brown and a toothpick intserted in the center comes out clean.

7. Let the cake cool on the counter. When cool, cut into 12 squares for serving.

VARIATIONS

If you like this cake and want to change it a bit, throw in these additions at the end just before pouring into the baking pan.

½ cup finely chopped nuts, such as (60 g) walnuts or (55 g) pecans
½ cup chopped dried fruit, such as (75 g) raisins or (89 g) dates

Vegan Vanilla Cupcakes with Coconut Whipped Cream

Makes 16 cupcakes

Sweetened with agave, these cupcakes are not just for vegans. They are moist, fluffy, and utterly delicious. Frost with Coconut Whipped Cream or eat them plain, as I do.

(V) (DF) (NF)

FOR THE CUPCAKES

1½ cups (188 g) all-purpose flour
1 teaspoon baking soda
1 teaspoon baking powder
½ teaspoon sea salt
1 cup (235 ml) rice milk
¾ cup (240 g) agave
½ cup (120 ml) safflower oil
1 tablespoon (15 ml) apple cider vinegar
2 teaspoons vanilla extract

FOR THE COCONUT WHIPPED CREAM

1 can (13.5 ounces, or 380 ml) full-fat coconut milk (or 1 small can of plain coconut cream)
2 tablespoons (26 g) sugar or (12 g) sugar substitute powder

1. A night or a few hours before you want to make this, chill the can of coconut milk in the fridge and leave it there until you are ready to make this recipe.

2. Preheat the oven to 350°F (180°C, or gas mark 4).

3. In a large bowl, add the all-purpose flour, baking soda, baking powder, and sea salt. Gently combine with a spoon.

4. Add the rice milk, agave, safflower oil, apple cider vinegar, and vanilla extract to your blender container. Blend a few seconds until smooth and well combined.

5. Add the flour mixture to the blender container and use a spoon to quickly distribute the mixture. Blend for just a few seconds until combined, but be careful to not overblend.

6. Pour or ladle the batter into silicone baking cups or muffin pans with paper cupcake liners about ¾ full.

7. Bake for 15 to 20 minutes until brown on top and a toothpick inserted in the center comes out clean.

8. To make the Coconut Whipped Cream: Remove the can of chilled coconut milk from your fridge, being careful not to shake it. Open the can with a can opener and gently scoop out the cream portion that has risen to the top of the can. Be careful to not remove any of the coconut milk liquid. Add it to your blender container with the sugar. Blend until smooth and the mixture begins to stiffen. Chill the whipped cream in the refrigerator to thicken. For best results, allow it to chill for at least 2 hours.

9. Frost the cooled cupcakes with the thickened whipped cream just before serving. The whipped cream must be chilled at all times or it melts.

Flourless Walnut Fudge Brownies

Makes 16 squares

If you adore brownies, but prefer a healthier version without gluten, give this recipe a try. These are super moist and gooey. I promise you'll be in heaven after one bite.

GF

6 tablespoons (85 g) softened unsalted butter
10 ounces (280 g) semisweet chocolate chips, about 1½ cups
¾ cup (108 g) coconut sugar
3 whole eggs
2 teaspoons vanilla extract
⅓ cup (43 g) arrowroot powder
¼ cup (20 g) cocoa powder
½ teaspoon ground cinnamon
½ teaspoon sea salt
1 cup (120 g) chopped walnut pieces (optional)

1. Preheat the oven to 350°F (180°C, or gas mark 4). Lightly spray with oil or butter an 8 x 8-inch (20 x 20 cm) nonstick pan or glass baking dish. Line the bottom of the pan with parchment paper and then also spray or butter the parchment paper.

2. Melt the butter and chocolate chips in a small saucepan over low heat until mostly melted. Remove from the heat and stir with a spoon until smooth. Set aside.

3. Add the sugar, eggs, and vanilla in your blender container. Blend until smooth.

4. Add the butter-and-chocolate mixture, arrowroot, cocoa powder, cinnamon, and sea salt. Blend until smooth, using the tamper or stopping to scrape down the sides with a spatula. The batter will be thick.

5. Add in the walnut pieces (if using) and gently stir to combine the nuts into the batter.

6. Pour the batter into the pan. Bake for 30 to 35 minutes or until set, when a toothpick inserted in the center comes out with a few crumbs, but is not completely clean.

7. Cool for 10 minutes and then remove the brownies from the pan with the parchment paper onto a cutting board. Let cool for an additional 10 minutes. Cut into 16 squares.

Coconut Caramel Freezer Fudge

Makes about 1½ cups (355 ml) fudge batter or sixteen 1-inch (2.5 cm) fudge squares

This healthy freezer fudge can be made in about 10 minutes. It's also vegan, low-sugar, gluten-free, and absolutely decadent. It's perfect if you are trying to cut out all refined sugar in your diet, but still want sweets. You can use any type of extract to enhance your fudge, but the best flavors to use with this recipe are vanilla, lemon, coconut, or caramel flavors. If you're not a fan of stevia extract, omit it and add more maple syrup to taste—it naturally brings out the caramel flavor.

(V) (GF) (DF) (NF)

¾ cup (168 g) coconut oil
4 cups (240 g) unsweetened coconut flakes
½ teaspoon vanilla extract
½ teaspoon caramel extract
½ tablespoon maple syrup
½ teaspoon liquid stevia extract

1. Add the coconut oil, coconut flakes, vanilla, caramel extract, maple syrup, and stevia extract to your blender.

2. Blend on a low to medium speed, using the tamper or stopping to scrape down the sides to redistribute the mixture. Blend until it becomes a coconut butter consistency. The mixture will be thick and takes a few minutes of blending.

3. Scoop the batter into a greased loaf pan and press it in so it's a completely even layer. Alternatively, transfer the batter into silicone candy molds.

4. Refrigerate for about 1 hour until firm. To speed up the chill time, place it in the freezer for 15 to 30 minutes.

5. Cut the fudge into 1-inch (2.5 cm) squares and store in the refrigerator for up to a week.

☞ **SERVING TIP**

If you're having a party or want to make these look fancy, line the bottom of the loaf pan or candy molds with chocolate gratings, sprinkles, chopped nuts, or coconut flakes before pouring the batter into the loaf pan. When you turn them over, the top will show the decorative add-ins.

Carrot Cupcakes with Chocolate Drizzle

Makes 15 cupcakes

Carrot cupcakes usually don't have a chocolate drizzle, but trust me on this one, it's fantastic. These cupcakes are not overly sweet but just right. If you prefer making a cake instead of cupcakes, bake it in a 9 x 13-inch (23 x 33 cm) nonstick pan for 30 minutes.

FOR THE CUPCAKES

3 large carrots, cut into chunks
4 whole eggs
1 cup (235 ml) grapeseed oil
1¾ cups (350 g) sugar or (252 g) coconut
  sugar
1 cup (120 g) spelt flour
1 cup (125 g) all-purpose flour
1 teaspoon baking powder

FOR THE CHOCOLATE DRIZZLE

2 tablespoons (28 g) softened butter
2 tablespoons (10 g) unsweetened cocoa
  powder
2 tablespoons (18 g) coconut sugar
3 tablespoons (45 ml) almond milk

1. Preheat the oven to 375°F (190°C, or gas mark 5).

2. Add the carrots, eggs, and oil to your blender container. Blend until smooth.

3. In a large bowl, add the sugar, spelt flour, all-purpose flour, and baking powder. Gently stir with a spoon to combine ingredients.

4. Pour the blender mixture in the bowl with the flour mixture and with a spoon, stir until well combined and smooth. Don't overmix.

5. Fill muffin pans lined with silicone baking cups or paper muffin cups lightly sprayed with oil ¾ full. Bake for 15 minutes or until a toothpick inserted in the center comes out clean. Let cool.

6. Meanwhile, to make the chocolate drizzle: Add the butter, cocoa powder, milk, and sugar to a small saucepan. Heat over medium-low heat while stirring until melted and combined.

7. Place the cupcakes on a cooling rack. Prick each cupcake with a fork. Using a spoon, drizzle about ½ teaspoon of the chocolate drizzle over each cupcake.

Raw Strawberry Cheesecake

Makes 1 cheesecake, about 8 slices

This amazing dessert is silky smooth and just like cheesecake, but it's surprisingly dairy-free. The cheesecake mixture will melt at room temperature because of the coconut oil, so be sure to leave it in the refrigerator at all times when not serving. Top the cheesecake with fresh strawberries and raspberries for a beautiful, two-toned, pink-hued dessert. I prefer to use honey in this recipe but agave works well, too.

GF **DF**

FOR THE CRUST

1 cup (100 g) raw walnuts
¼ cup (15 g) unsweetened coconut flakes
⅛ teaspoon sea salt

FOR THE CHEESECAKE

2 cups (340 g) fresh chopped strawberries
1 cup (140 g) raw cashews
1 tablespoon (15 ml) vanilla extract
½ cup (170 g) raw honey or agave
⅛ teaspoon sea salt
1 cup (224 g) coconut oil
Sliced strawberries and raspberries,
 for garnish

1. To make the crust, place the walnuts, coconut flakes, and sea salt in your blender container. Blend on high until combined, but still crumbly.

2. Scoop the mixture out onto a 9-inch (23 cm) pie plate and press it into the bottom of the plate, but not up the sides. Alternatively, use a springform pan. Set aside.

3. To make the cheesecake, add the strawberries, cashews, vanilla, honey, sea salt, and coconut oil to your blender container.

4. Blend until completely combined, smooth, and creamy. It will be runny.

5. Pour the mixture on top of the crust. Transfer the plate to the refrigerator and let cool overnight or for at least 6 hours.

6. When firm, garnish with strawberries and raspberries before cutting into slices. Keep chilled at all times to avoid melting.

Cinnamon Applesauce

Makes 2 cups (490 g)

Applesauce sans white sugar is hard to find unless you make it yourself. This version uses medjool dates which add vitamins and sweetness. It's great for dessert, and it's fantastic served as a snack or as a sweet side to dinner entrees.

V **GF** **DF** **NF**

5 pitted medjool dates, chopped
3 large apples, any variety, cored and
  chopped
¼ cup (60 ml) lemon juice
¼ teaspoon cinnamon

1. Add the dates, apples, lemon juice, and cinnamon to your blender container.

2. Blend on low speed until combined and then blend high until well combined and smooth. Serve. Leftovers can be refrigerated for up to one week.

Gluten-Free Coconut Custard Cake Bars

Makes twelve 3-inch (7.5 cm) bars

These cake bars are to die for. They have a creamy, sweet layer on the inside, and they cut well into squares for easy finger desserts. This recipe is also gluten-free, and I promise you won't be able to tell, making it great for a crowd with some guests that have sensitivities. Serve squares in individual colorful paper baking cups spread on a large tray for a creative party dessert. There's no need to serve these warm; they taste great cold.

GF **NF**

1 can (13 ounces, or 365 ml) of full-fat unsweetened coconut milk
1½ cups (355 ml) milk, any variety
3 whole eggs
1 tablespoon (14 g) softened butter
1½ cups (300 g) sugar
1 cup (136 g) 1 to 1 gluten-free all-purpose flour mix, such as Bob's Red Mill
½ cup (50 g) grated Parmesan cheese
1 tablespoon (14 g) baking powder

1. Preheat the oven to 350°F (180°C, or gas mark 4). Lightly oil, spray, or grease and flour a 9 x 13-inch (23 x 33 cm) pan or glass baking dish.

2. Add the coconut milk, milk, eggs, butter, sugar, gluten-free flour, Parmesan cheese, and baking powder to your blender container and blend on high until well combined.

3. Pour the batter in baking dish and use a silicone spatula to even out the mixture.

4. Bake for 40 minutes until golden brown on top and a toothpick inserted in the center comes out clean.

5. Cool completely on the counter. When cool, cut into 12 squares.

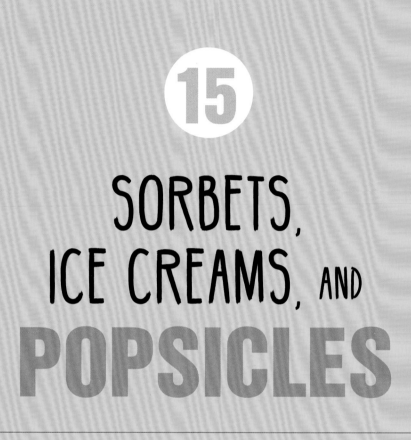

15

SORBETS, ICE CREAMS, AND POPSICLES

A power blender is ideal for making easy desserts like ice creams, sorbets, and popsicles. Not only can you make them quickly, you can control the ingredients and sugar content to make healthy, guilt-free snacks that everyone will love.

Strawberry Sorbet ▶

Makes 4 servings

Once you taste this, you'll have a hard time believing it has only three ingredients. It's naturally sweet and delicious all on its own with no added sugar or unnecessary dairy. Strawberries are high on the antioxidant list and low on the glycemic index.

(V) (GF) (DF) (NF) (LS)

16 ounces (455 g) frozen strawberries (about 4 cups)
1½ cups (355 ml) water, plus more if needed
20 drops of liquid stevia extract, or more to taste

1. Add the frozen strawberries, water, and stevia extract to your blender container.

2. Pulse to get the mixture moving and then blend on high until it reaches a smooth, sorbet-like consistency and has stiff mounds. You may have to stop and scrape the sides down or use a tamper to push the strawberries into the blades. Add more water, a few tablespoons (45 ml) at a time, if needed to process.

3. Taste and add more stevia extract, if you'd like. This is best served immediately.

☞ TIP

Using already frozen bagged from the store fruit saves time in the kitchen. Leave bags of frozen fresh fruit in your freezer to make quick sorbets when sweet cravings hit.

Mixed Berry Sorbet

Makes 2 servingss

If you have frozen berries in your freezer, this dessert cannot get any quicker. It's perfect for a very quick sweet treat. If you have blood sugar problems or are on a low-carb diet, this is an ideal dessert for you to try. This berry mix is only lightly sweetened, so it's perfect for you if you don't like overly sweet sorbets.

1 cup (155 g) frozen blueberries
2 cups (298 g) frozen strawberries
1 cup (235 ml) water
1 teaspoon vanilla extract
1 tablespoon (20 g) honey or agave, or more to taste
5 drops of liquid stevia extract

1. Add the blueberries, strawberries, water, vanilla, honey or agave, and stevia extract to your blender container.

2. Pulse to get the mixture moving and then blend on high until it reaches a smooth, sorbet-like consistency. You may have to stop and scrape the sides down or use the tamper. Add more water, a few tablespoons (15 ml) at a time, if needed to process.

3. Taste and add more stevia extract, honey, or agave if you'd like. This is best served immediately.

Pineapple Whip Sorbet

Makes 2 serving

Pineapple is naturally sweet and makes for an amazing sorbet dessert. I love this topped with Coconut Whipped Cream (page 250) and a little Dark Chocolate Sauce (page 146). It's also great on its own, especially on a hot summer day.

8 ounces (about 2 cups or 310 g) pineapple, rind removed, chopped and frozen
1 cup (235 ml) water
10 drops of liquid stevia extract, or more to taste

1. Add the pineapple, water, and stevia extract to your blender container.

2. Pulse to get the mixture moving and then blend on high until it reaches a smooth, sorbet-like consistency. You may have to stop and scrape the sides down or use the tamper. Add more water, a few tablespoons (45 ml) at a time, if needed to process.

3. Taste and add more stevia extract, if you'd like. This is best served immediately.

VARIATION: Add 1 chopped and frozen ripe banana to these ingredients to make this a creamier, thicker pineapple whip.

◄ Vegan Banana Whip

Makes 2 servings

This was one of the first desserts I made with my high-powered blender and if you've never made it, it's time. This is hands down the best vegan and dairy-free version of ice cream I can imagine. I'm constantly amazed at the creamy, fine texture that is so close to regular ice cream.

2 bananas, peeled and frozen in 1-inch
  (2.5 cm) chunks
1 cup (235 ml) almond, coconut, or rice
  milk, plus more if needed
1 teaspoon vanilla extract

1. Add the bananas, almond milk, and vanilla to your blender container.

2. Pulse to get the mixture moving and then blend on high until it reaches a smooth, sorbet-like consistency. You may have to stop and scrape the sides down or use the tamper. Add more almond milk, a few tablespoons (45 ml) at a time, if needed to process.

3. This is best served immediately.

☞ **BLENDING TIP**

If you like making banana ice creams, keep frozen banana chunks in the freezer for a quick and easy dessert. To do this, peel and chop up several bananas into ½- to 1-inch (about 1 to 2 cm) chunks. This size is ideal for the blender to handle. Wrap the chunks in parchment paper and store them in a large plastic bag in the freezer until ready to use. They will break apart easily for blending.

VARIATION: If you like the flavor of malt desserts, powdered maca powder tastes surprisingly similar and is an herb that is used to combat stress and fatigue. Try making this a malted milk ball flavored whip sundae by adding in 1 tablespoon (5 g) of maca powder to the ingredients before blending, transfer to a bowl, and add 1 to 2 tablespoons (11 to 22 g) of chocolate chips and a drizzle of Dark Chocolate Sauce (page 146) to the top.

Mango and Coconut Cream Sorbet

Makes 1 serving

Mangoes are great for your complexion and antioxidant intake. So, why not amp up your nutrition with a dessert? Mango is ideal for making sorbet because it has a nice creamy texture when blended with coconut milk. This will be your favorite go-to when mango is in season.

2 cups (350 g) mango chunks, peeled and frozen
¼ cup (60 ml) full-fat canned coconut milk, plus more if needed
15 drops of liquid stevia extract

1. Add the frozen mango, coconut milk, and stevia extract to your blender container.

2. Pulse to get the mixture moving and then blend on high until it reaches a smooth, sorbet-like consistency. You may have to stop and scrape the sides down or use the tamper. Add more coconut milk, a few tablespoons (45 ml) at a time, if needed to process.

3. Taste and add more stevia extract, if you'd like. This is best served immediately.

☞ **BLENDING TIP**

If you want to freeze soft fruit like papayas and melons for quick frozen desserts, use a melon baller instead of a knife to achieve consistent size chunks, as this small size is ideal for the blender to handle.

Peanut Butter Banana Whip

Makes 2 servings

The first time I had a banana whip was at a seaside café in New Jersey. Since then, I've made them regularly and easily in my power blender. This peanut butter version is highly addictive. Once you have a bite, you won't be sharing!

2 bananas, peeled and frozen in 1-inch (2.5 cm) chunks
2 tablespoons (32 g) natural creamy peanut butter
½ cup (120 ml) almond milk
½ tablespoon maple syrup, plus more to taste

1. Add the bananas, peanut butter, almond milk, and maple syrup to your blender container.

2. Pulse to get the mixture moving and then blend on high until it reaches a smooth, sorbet-like consistency. You may have to stop and scrape the sides down or use the tamper. Add more almond milk, a few tablespoons (45 ml) at a time, if needed to process.

3. Taste and add more maple syrup, if you'd like. This is best served immediately.

☞ **SERVING TIP**

To make a peanut butter and jelly sundae that is divine, layer the peanut butter banana whip with the Strawberry Sorbet (page 258), in an ice cream sundae cup. It makes the perfect healthy dessert.

Vegan Mint Chip Ice Cream

Makes 1 serving

This ice cream uses zucchini and banana as the base for a lighter style banana whip, but you'd never know it. I often add 1 to 2 scoops of vanilla protein powder to the mixture and make this for a post-workout alternative to a protein shake—because I'll take ice cream over a shake, any day.

¼ cup (60 ml) coconut milk
1 frozen banana, peeled and chopped
1 cup (120 g) zucchini, chopped and frozen
½ teaspoon vanilla extract
½ teaspoon mint extract
2 tablespoons (22 g) chocolate chips

1. Place the coconut milk, banana, zucchini, vanilla, and mint extract in your blender container.

2. Pulse or blend on low to get the mixture moving and then blend on high until smooth and well combined, using the tamper and stopping to scrape down the sides. The mixture will be thick. Add more coconut milk, a few tablespoons (45 ml) at a time, if needed to process.

3. Transfer to a bowl and mix in the chocolate chips with a spoon. This is best served immediately. This ice cream will not keep well in the freezer.

☞ **SERVING TIP**

Add additional toppings for a luxurious ice cream sundae. Top with toasted coconut, Dark Chocolate Sauce (page 146), or walnuts.

Chocolate Mocha Fudge Popsicles

Makes 6 popsicles

Chocolate lovers, this one's for you! These fudgy popsicles taste so luscious you won't believe they're super healthy and made with avocado. Make a batch of these to keep on hand because everyone who sees you with one will want one, too.

1½ cups (355 ml) full-fat coconut milk
½ cup (40 g) cocoa powder
5 tablespoons (100 g) maple syrup
1 large avocado, pitted and peeled
1 tablespoon (4 g) instant espresso powder

1. Add the coconut milk, cocoa powder, maple syrup, avocado, and espresso powder to your blender container.

2. Blend until smooth and creamy.

3. Pour the mixture into ice pop molds. Place the mold coverings on top. Freeze overnight.

4. To serve, run the molds under hot water to loosen the popsicles, if needed.

Coconut Lime Popsicles

Makes 6 popsicles

These beautifully green pops are full of vitamins and completely free of refined sugar. You'll never believe you got such good-for-you ingredients into a delicious ice pop! If you like texture in your pops, add ¼ cup (20 g) of shredded coconut flakes to the batter before pouring it in the molds.

V **GF** **DF** **NF**

1 large Hass avocado, about 1 cup (230 g) mashed
1 cup (235 ml) unsweetened canned full-fat coconut milk
⅓ cup (80 ml) fresh lime juice
⅓ cup (107 g) maple syrup

1. Add the avocado, coconut milk, lime juice, and maple syrup to your blender container.

2. Blend until completely smooth.

3. Remove the blender container from the base and add in the coconut flakes (if using; see above). Gently stir in the flakes until combined.

4. Pour the mixture into ice pop molds. Place the mold covering on top. Freeze overnight.

5. To serve, run the molds under hot water to loosen the popsicles, if needed.

Watermelon Popsicles

Makes 6 popsicles

The perfect summertime picnic treat, watermelon popsicles take just a few minutes to make. They are naturally sweet and hydrating, just like you'd expect.

V **GF** **DF** **NF** **LS**

3 cups (450 g) seedless watermelon, cubed, rind removed
2 tablespoons (28 ml) lemon juice
20 drops of liquid stevia extract, or more to taste

1. Place the watermelon, lemon juice, and stevia extract in your blender container.

2. Blend until completely combined and smooth.

3. Taste and add more stevia extract, if you'd like.

4. Pour the mixture into ice pop molds. Place the mold coverings on top. Freeze overnight.

5. To serve, run the molds under hot water to loosen the popsicles, if needed.

Peach Ice Cream

Makes 2 cups (280 g)

This ice cream is more like traditional varieties. It uses milk which makes a very creamy and flavorful dessert. Because I don't like using an ice cream maker to make ice cream, this ice cream is just one step and so much easier than pulling out that big machine. Don't allow the peaches to defrost before blending.

1 cup (235 ml) whole milk, plus more if needed
1½ tablespoons (20 g) sugar or (14 g) coconut sugar
1 teaspoon vanilla extract
2 cups (340 g) peaches, skin removed, chopped and frozen

1. Add the milk, sugar, vanilla, and peaches to your blender container.

2. Pulse to get the mixture moving and then blend on high until it reaches a smooth, ice cream–like consistency. You may have to stop and scrape the sides down. Add more milk, a few tablespoons (45 ml) at a time, if needed to process. Add more frozen peaches if you want it thicker. It will be thick and the machine will fight to blend. (This is normal.)

3. This ice cream is best served immediately.

Vanilla Ice Cream

Makes 1 cup (140 g)

If you've ever had a craving for vanilla ice cream, but you don't want to wait for your ice cream machine, I have your answer! Ice cream that's rich and creamy in your blender is possible, in just minutes. I know you don't believe me, so you'll have to try it out for yourself. This makes enough for one nice bowl of ice cream. If you want to share, you'll have to double the recipe.

1 cup (235 ml) heavy whipping cream
1 tablespoon (15 ml) vanilla extract
¼ cup (50 g) sugar or (36 g) coconut sugar
1 tablespoon (20 g) honey

1. Add the heavy whipping cream, vanilla, sugar, and honey to your blender container.

2. Blend on high until completely combined.

3. Pour into an ice cube tray and freeze for at least 8 hours or overnight. This mixture will fit an entire standard ice cube tray. When frozen, remove the cubes from the tray and add them to your blender container.

4. Blend until it reaches an ice cream–like consistency, using the tamper or stopping to scrape down the sides.

5. This is best served immediately.

Double Chocolate Ice Cream

Makes 1 cup (140 g)

This really should be named "Chocolate Overload Ice Cream" because it's bursting with layers of chocolate flavor that whirl your taste buds into a tailspin. This recipe is so close to an ice cream machine's version, you'll be hard-pressed to find someone who thinks different. So go ahead and try to fool them. To make this dessert even more decadent, add a drizzle of Salted Date Caramel Sauce (page 147).

(GF) (NF)

1 cup (235 ml) half-and-half
¼ cup (50 g) sugar or (36 g) coconut sugar
1 teaspoon vanilla extract
¼ cup (20 g) unsweetened cocoa powder
¼ cup (44 g) mini chocolate chips

1. Add the half-and-half, sugar, vanilla, and cocoa powder to your blender container.

2. Blend on high until completely combined.

3. Pour the ice cream into an ice cube tray and freeze for at least 8 hours or overnight. This mixture will fit an entire standard ice cube tray. When frozen, remove the cubes from the tray and add them to your blender container.

4. Blend until it reaches an ice cream–like consistency, using the tamper or stopping to scrape down the sides.

5. Add the chocolate chips and using a spatula, gently stir to combine, working quickly to avoid melting. This is best served immediately.

Orange Cream Frozen Yogurt

Makes 1½ cups (370 g)

I find it exciting that I can make my own soft serve frozen yogurt at home without a complicated process. This will take two days to make because you'll have to freeze your yogurt first, but it's well worth it. Silicone ice cube trays are my favorite for making the work easier when it comes time to remove them from the tray. Use any plain yogurt you'd like, but I prefer whole milk yogurt varieties because they have a richer flavor.

GF **NF**

2 cups (230 g) frozen plain Greek yogurt, whole milk, 2%, or fat-free
½ cup plus 2 tablespoons (150 ml) fresh or store-bought orange juice, plus more if needed
1½ tablespoons (30 g) honey

1. A day before you'd like to enjoy this yogurt, pour the yogurt into ice cube trays and freeze.

2. To make the frozen yogurt: Add the orange juice, frozen Greek yogurt cubes, and honey to your blender container. Blend until smooth and all the yogurt cubes have been combined, using the tamper to push the cubes into the blades.

3. Add more orange juice if needed to process. This is best served immediately.

Vegan Cherry Vanilla Frozen Yogurt

Makes 1 cup (245 g)

Dairy-free frozen yogurt is easy to make when you have any variety of nondairy yogurt on hand. Tart cherry adds just the right amount of flavor to make a silky-smooth ice cream treat. Eat this on its own or make an ice cream sandwich by putting the frozen yogurt between two vegan sugar cookies and freezing. Double the recipe if you want to share.

V **GF** **NF**

1 cup (230 g) vanilla coconut yogurt or soy yogurt
¼ cup (60 ml) tart cherry juice, plus more if needed
1 teaspoon vanilla extract
2 tablespoons (40 g) agave

1. A day before you'd like to enjoy this yogurt, pour the yogurt into an ice cube tray and freeze.

2. To make the frozen yogurt: Add the tart cherry juice, frozen yogurt cubes, vanilla, and agave to your blender container. Blend until smooth and all the yogurt cubes have been combined, using the tamper to push the cubes into the blades.

3. Add more cherry juice if needed to process. This is best served immediately.

16

BABY FOOD
PURÉES

Making your own baby food is often more economical and healthier because you can control the ingredients. You'll be happy to know that you can do this quick and easy with your trusty power blender by your side. Purchase little glass jars and make a batch of food each week. You'll save yourself time and money, and you'll ensure you are feeding your baby the best.

Carrot Puree

Makes 1 to 2 cups (245 to 490 g)

Carrots are high in beta carotene which is important to an infant's diet. Carrots are also naturally sweet and pleasant tasting. Use only whole raw carrots and not pre-peeled, precut baby carrots, as they are washed in a solution you might want to avoid for the purest food.

(V) (GF) (DF) (NF) (LS)

2 cups (260 g) chopped peeled carrots
1½ cups (355 ml) filtered water

1. In a saucepan, combine the carrots and water. Bring to a boil, reduce the heat, and let simmer uncovered for 15 minutes until the carrots are soft. Let sit for 5 minutes to cool.

2. Transfer the carrots and water to your blender container. Process until smooth, using the tamper or stopping to scrape down the sides, if necessary. Thin the mixture out with more water to reach the desired consistency, if needed.

3. Let cool to store or serve immediately at room temperature. Refrigerate for up to 24 hours in small glass jars or another airtight container. For freezing, pour the puree into equally distributed ice cube trays, cover with plastic wrap, and freeze until solid. Once frozen, transfer the cubes to freezer bags or small jars. Store in the freezer for up to 2 months. Thaw the cubes in the refrigerator overnight or for at least 5 hours before serving.

☞ **TIP**

Baby food can be stored in the freezer for up to 2 months. When ready to use, thaw the cubes in the refrigerator overnight or at least 5 hours and serve.

Carrot and Apple Puree ▶

Makes 1 to 2 cups (245 to 490 g)

Carrots and apples provide key nutrients for your baby, along with a good amount of fiber. I think you'll find this simple mixture will be a winner with your little one, and it's easy for you to make often. There's no need to peel the apple; the blender will ensure that all the peels are mixed in perfectly.

(V) (GF) (DF) (NF) (LS)

1 cup (130 g) peeled carrots
1 cup (125 g) chopped unpeeled apple
1½ cups (355 ml) filtered water

1. In a saucepan, combine the carrots, apples, and water. Bring to a boil, reduce the heat, and let simmer uncovered for 15 minutes until the carrots and apples are very soft. Let sit for 5 minutes to cool.

2. Transfer the carrot-and-apple mixture and the water to your blender container. Process until smooth, using the tamper or stopping to scrape down the sides, if necessary. Thin the mixture out with more water to reach the desired consistency, if needed.

3. Let cool to store or serve immediately at room temperature. Refrigerate for up to 24 hours in small glass jars or another airtight container. For freezing, pour the puree into equally distributed ice cube trays, cover with plastic wrap, and freeze until solid. Once frozen, transfer the cubes to freezer bags or small jars. Store in the freezer for up to 2 months. Thaw the cubes in the refrigerator overnight or for at least 5 hours before serving.

Sweet Potato Puree

Makes 1 to 2 cups (245 to 490 g)

Sweet potatoes are a powerhouse of nutrients and loaded with fiber. It takes a little bit longer to chop and cook the sweet potatoes, but it's worth it for the nutrients.

(V) (GF) (DF) (NF) (LS)

2 cups (266 g) chopped peeled sweet
  potatoes
2 cups (475 ml) filtered water, divided

1. In a saucepan, combine the sweet potatoes and 1 cup (235 ml) of water. Bring to a boil, reduce the heat, and let simmer uncovered for 20 minutes until the sweet potatoes are very soft. Let sit for 5 minutes to cool.

2. Transfer the sweet potatoes and water to your blender container. Process until smooth, using the tamper or stopping to scrape down the sides, if necessary. Thin the mixture out with more water to reach the desired consistency, if needed.

3. Let cool to store or serve immediately at room temperature. Refrigerate for up to 24 hours in small glass jars or another airtight container. For freezing, pour the puree into equally distributed ice cube trays, cover with plastic wrap, and freeze until solid. Once frozen, transfer the cubes to freezer bags or small jars. Store in the freezer for up to 2 months. Thaw the cubes in the refrigerator overnight or for at least 5 hours before serving.

Pea and Spinach Puree

Makes 1 to 2 cups (245 to 490 g)

If you think your baby won't like this, try it and you might be surprised. Green peas are naturally sweet, which helps to mask the flavor of spinach.

1 cup (130 g) frozen green peas
3 cups (90 g) lightly packed spinach
1½ cups (355 ml) filtered water

1. In a saucepan, combine the peas and water. Bring to a boil, reduce the heat, and let simmer for 10 minutes. Add the spinach and simmer uncovered for an additional 5 minutes until the peas and spinach are very soft and cooked through. Let sit for 5 minutes to cool.

2. Transfer the peas and spinach, with the water, to your blender container. Process until smooth. Thin the mixture out with more water to reach the desired consistency, if needed.

3. Let cool to store or serve immediately at room temperature. Refrigerate for up to 24 hours in small glass jars or another airtight container. For freezing, pour the puree into equally distributed ice cube trays, cover with plastic wrap, and freeze until solid. Once frozen, transfer the cubes to freezer bags or small jars and store in the freezer for up to 2 months. Thaw the cubes in the refrigerator overnight or for at least 5 hours before serving.

Chicken and Kale Puree

Makes 1 to 2 cups (245 to 490 g)

Kale is high in calcium, and it pairs perfectly with chicken for a protein and iron rich meal.

1½ cups (about 260 g) chicken breast cut into 1-inch (2.5 cm) pieces
2 cups (134 g) lightly packed baby kale leaves
1½ cups (355 ml) filtered water

1. In a saucepan, combine the chicken and water. Bring to a boil, reduce the heat, and let simmer uncovered for 15 to 20 minutes until the chicken is cooked through. Add the kale and simmer for an additional 5 minutes. Let sit for 5 minutes to cool.

2. Transfer the chicken-and-kale mixture, with the water, to your blender container. Process until smooth. Thin the mixture out with more water to reach the desired consistency, if needed.

3. Let cool to store or serve immediately at room temperature. Refrigerate for up to 24 hours in an airtight container. For freezing, pour the puree into ice cube trays, cover with plastic wrap, and freeze until solid. Once frozen, transfer the cubes to freezer bags or small jars and store in the freezer for up to 2 months. Thaw the cubes in the refrigerator overnight or for at least 5 hours before serving.

Banana Avocado Puree

Makes 1 to 2 cups (245 to 490 g)

This is one of the easiest, most classic meals to give your infant because there's no need to cook this banana avocado mixture. It's also naturally tasty and full of healthy fats. This doesn't refrigerate or freeze as well as other baby foods, so I recommend making this on demand as you need it.

1 large ripe peeled banana, broken in chunks
1 large peeled and pitted avocado
2 to 4 tablespoons (28 to 60 ml) filtered water

1. Add the banana, avocado, and water to your blender container. Process until smooth, using the tamper or stopping to scrape down the sides, if necessary. Thin the mixture out with more water to reach the desired consistency, if needed.

2. Serve immediately or refrigerate for up to 12 hours in small glass jars or another airtight container.

1 cup (161 g) chopped unpeeled pear
2 cups (240 g) chopped zucchini
1¾ cups (410 ml) filtered water

1. In a saucepan, combine the pear, zucchini, and water. Bring to a boil, reduce the heat, and let simmer uncovered for 15 minutes until the pears and zucchini are very soft. Let sit for 5 minutes to cool.

2. Transfer the pear-and-zucchini mixture, with the water, to your blender container. Process until smooth, using the tamper or stopping to scrape down the sides, if necessary. Thin the mixture out with more water to reach the desired consistency, if needed.

3. Let cool to store or serve immediately at room temperature. Refrigerate for up to 24 hours in small glass jars or another airtight container. For freezing, pour the puree into equally distributed ice cube trays, cover with plastic wrap, and freeze until solid. Once frozen, transfer the cubes to freezer bags or small jars. Store in the freezer for up to 2 months. Thaw the cubes in the refrigerator overnight or for at least 5 hours before serving.

▲ Pear Zucchini Puree

Makes 1 to 2 cups (245 to 490 g)

Pears are a great fruit to relieve baby's constipation, and they're gentle on the tummy. Adding nutrient-rich zucchini in the mix is a great combination and sure to be a winner with your little one. If your baby has digestion issues, you might want to peel the zucchini, otherwise, the blender will blend it smoothly into the mix removing any lumps.

17

MASKS, WASHES, AND MORE FOR YOUR SKIN

Skincare products can often be pricey and filled with chemicals we'd rather not put on our bodies. Here's the good news! It's easy to make your own and indulge in spa-like products. These DIY skincare blends can be whipped up quickly in your kitchen and might do wonders for your skin. In my experience, nothing comes close to the powerful ingredients that nature provides to hydrate skin and restore a healthy glow. Permission granted: enjoy a spa night in the comfort of your own home.

Grapefruit Body Wash

Makes about ¾ cup (about 175 ml)

This effortless body wash can also double as your hand soap. I love the bright and cheery scent that grapefruit lends to this mixture.

¼ cup (60 ml) almond oil
½ cup (120 ml) unscented liquid castile soap
1 tablespoon (15 ml) vitamin E oil
15 drops of grapefruit essential oil

1. Add the almond oil, castile soap, vitamin E, and grapefruit oil to your blender container.

2. Blend until completely combined. Store in any glass or plastic bottle.

Honey Face Wash

Makes about 2 cups (about 475 ml)

Honey is an amazing ingredient to use on your skin because it has naturally antibacterial and calming properties. This face wash creates a nice lather and is super gentle for your delicate facial skin.

½ cup (120 ml) unscented liquid castile soap
½ cup (170 g) honey
4 tablespoons (60 ml) water
4 tablespoons (60 ml) jojoba oil

1. Add the castile soap, honey, water, and jojoba oil to your blender container.

2. Blend until completely combined. Store in any glass or plastic bottle.

Chamomile Oat Body Scrub

Makes about ½ cup (120 ml)

An easy and cheap way to exfoliate, this calming oat scrub has only three ingredients. The oats are a great gentle scrubber while the chamomile is a highly calming herb to help with any irritation. It will make your skin smooth in no time.

1 cup (96 g) old-fashioned rolled oats
¼ cup (56 g) coconut oil
½ cup (120 ml) brewed chamomile tea

1. Add the whole oats to your blender container. Blend until it becomes a fine powder.

2. Add the coconut oil and blend quickly to combine.

3. Add the brewed tea to the mixture. Pulse until combined.

4. Transfer the mixture to a glass wide mouth jar with a lid. Use small amounts of the scrub to gently exfoliate your skin.

Vanilla Body Lotion

Makes about 4 ounces (about 120 ml)

One great thing about your blender is that it can gently heat your mixture so you can avoid using the stove. Coconut oil is solid at room temperature. Once you add it to your blender with these other ingredients, you'll notice it will easily become liquid. This vanilla lotion is best used on the body and smells heavenly. Feel free to add in your favorite essential oils to enhance the benefits and scent.

½ cup (60 ml) jojoba oil
¼ cup (56 g) coconut oil
1 tablespoon (15 ml) vitamin E
1 teaspoon vanilla extract

1. Add the jojoba oil, coconut oil, vitamin E, and vanilla to your blender container.

2. Blend until smooth and creamy.

3. Use as you would regular lotion. Store in an airtight glass container.

Avocado Oat Exfoliation Mask

Makes about ½ cup (90 ml)

Avocado is rich in healthy fats that naturally moisturize skin. It's also high in vitamin E. Combined with the exfoliating power of oats in this recipe, you have the perfect delicate polishing mask for clear, bright skin.

½ of an avocado, pitted and peeled
⅓ cup (22 g) old-fashioned rolled oats
¼ cup (60 ml) almond milk

1. Place the avocado, oats, and almond milk in your blender container.

2. Blend until the mask is a smooth, creamy paste.

3. With your hands, apply the mask to your face, avoiding the eye area. Leave on for 5 to 10 minutes and then rinse well with water, gently exfoliating while rinsing.

Skin-Brightening Kiwi and Lemon Facial Mask

Makes about 1 cup (230 g)

This beautiful mask will naturally lighten and brighten your face with the natural enzymes found in kiwi, lemon, and yogurt. One batch will keep about a week in the refrigerator.

2 kiwis, peeled and chopped in half
¼ cup (60 g) plain yogurt
1 tablespoon (15 ml) lemon juice
1 tablespoon (15 ml) almond oil

1. Add the kiwis, yogurt, lemon juice, and almond oil to your blender container.

2. Process until smooth and creamy.

3. With your hands, apply the mask to your face, avoiding the eye area. Leave on until dry and then rinse well with water.

Avocado Moisture Mask

Makes ½ cup (120 g), enough for 3 masks

Avocado is full of healthy fats that are not only good for eating, but wonderful skin nourishers. If your facial skin is feeling dry—or even if you have a dry patch on your elbow or knee—try using this extremely hydrating moisture mask to soothe it. If you only have a small avocado on hand, reduce the honey and coconut oil to 1 tablespoon each (20 g and 14 g) instead of 2 tablespoons (40 g and 28 g).

1 large avocado, pitted and peeled
1 egg yolk
2 tablespoons (40 g) honey
2 tablespoons (28 g) coconut oil

1. Add the avocado, egg yolk, honey, and coconut oil to your blender container.

2. Blend until smooth and creamy.

3. With your hands, apply the mask to your face, avoiding the eye area. Leave on for about 10 minutes and then rinse well with water.

ACKNOWLEDGMENTS

There have been so many people and experiences that have led to the wonderful creation of this book, and for that I'm grateful.

Adam, thanks for always taste testing my good and bad recipes and helping out in the kitchen—we'll never forget those mountains of dishes and maxed out fridges. Secondly, thank you for your amazing support, love, and kindness as I pursue my dreams and take on large projects. You've contributed so positively to my life journey, and I am so blessed to be your wife.

Mom, my eternal thanks go to you for teaching me how to cook, giving me ideas, testing my recipes, and offering up endless support and advice. I'm so lucky to have you in my life and love you very much. Dad, thank you for your support, your love, and for trying out my recipes. Thank you for everything.

To all of my friends, thank you for being in my life and making it better. Thank you for your support, ideas, and love as I produced this book. Your friendship means the world to me, and I'm grateful we've crossed paths in life.

Thanks to my agent Stacey Glick, my editor Dan Rosenberg, and everyone at Harvard Common Press and Quarto for making this book happen and doing it so well. Thank you for all of your hard work throughout this process.

To everyone in the Simkins and Lindeman families, I genuinely feel that I have the best family and appreciate how wonderfully supportive and loving you all are through my projects. I'm blessed to have you all in my life.

To all my *All About Juicing* fans, this work is for you and without you this book wouldn't have been possible. I'm flattered you've picked up this book and delighted that these recipes will be a part of your life. My dream is that this book will be helpful to you in many ways.

And to God, thank you for providing me the most amazing opportunities and the ability to follow through with them. I never would've dreamed all the things you've had in store for me and am overjoyed to be a vessel you use to help others.

ABOUT THE AUTHOR

Vanessa Simkins is the creator, writer, and photographer behind AllAboutJuicing.com, a popular website and newsletter that thousands of readers depend upon for fresh, reliable advice on how to juice for a fit and slim body, glowing skin, and lifelong health. She is also the author of *The Juice Lover's Big Book of Juices: 425 Recipes for Super Nutritious and Crazy Delicious Juices*. Vanessa lives in Austin, Texas, with her husband Adam.

INDEX